Key Issues in Bioethi

Young people are increasingly being exposed to the huge and complex ethical dilemmas involved in issues such as genetic modification, animal rights and cloning, and they are bringing their views into the classroom. But how can teachers be sure they are sufficiently well-informed to help their pupils make sense of the diverse and emotive arguments surrounding these issues?

This book may hold the answer. Written by leading ethicists, scientists and technologists, it offers a balanced and jargon-free guide to such highly debated topics as:

- Cloning
- *In vitro* fertilisation
- Genetic screening and genetic engineering
- Farm animal welfare
- The use of animals in medical experiments

Written specifically for the non-specialist teacher or lecturer, this book also contains suggestions on how to approach the teaching of bioethics and provides useful sources of further information.

Ralph Levinson is Lecturer in Science Education, Institute of Education, University of London. **Michael Reiss** is Professor of Science Education and Head of the School of Mathematics, Science and Technology, also at the Institute of Education.

Key Issues in Bioethics

A guide for teachers

Edited by
Ralph Levinson and
Michael J. Reiss

RoutledgeFalmer
Taylor & Francis Group

LONDON AND NEW YORK

First published 2003
by RoutledgeFalmer
11 New Fetter Lane, London EC4P 4EE

Simultaneously published in the USA and Canada
by RoutledgeFalmer
29 West 35th Street, New York, NY 10001

RoutledgeFalmer is an imprint of the Taylor & Francis Group

Typeset in Bembo by BC Typesetting, Bristol
Printed and bound in Great Britain by
MPG Books Ltd, Bodmin

British Library Cataloguing in Publication Data
A catalogue record for this book is available from the British Library

Library of Congress Cataloging in Publication Data
A catalogue record has been requested

ISBN 0–415–30914–X (hbk)
ISBN 0–415–27068–5 (pbk)

To Jenny Frost

Contents

Contributors

Bill Albert taught economic history at the University of East Anglia from 1968 to 1992. He has been active in the disability movement for about twenty years and currently chairs the Norfolk Coalition of Disabled People. He took the lead in drafting the British Council of Disabled People's position statement on disability and genetics as well as a similar statement from Disabled People's International Europe. He is a member of the UK government's Human Genetics Commission.

Elizabeth N. Anionwu is Professor of Nursing and head of the Mary Seacole Centre for Nursing Practice at Thames Valley University. Previously, she was head of the Brent Sickle and Thalassaemia Counselling Centre, the first to be established in Britain, and then organised over twenty 'Genetic Counselling for the Community' courses based at the Unit of Clinical Genetics and Fetal Medicine at the Institute of Child Health in London. Elizabeth is a member of the Human Genetics Commission and the Antenatal Screening subgroup of the National Screening Committee.

Rebecca Bennett is Lecturer in Bioethics and Fellow of the Institute of Medicine, Law and Bioethics. She is currently developing materials for the MA/Postgraduate Diploma in Health Care Ethics and Law by Distributed Learning. She has published widely on diverse issues in bioethics.

Joyce D'Silva has been Chief Executive of Compassion in World Farming (CIWF), the leading international organisation campaigning against factory farming, since 1991. Joyce has authored reports on several aspects of farm animal welfare from dairy cows to genetic engineering. She has also contributed to three books on genetic engineering and has addressed the issue at venues ranging from the Cambridge Union to the European Parliament's Intergroup on Animal Welfare. She also edits CIWF's flagship magazine, *Farm Animal Voice*. She says her personal aim is to end factory farming throughout the world, preferably in her lifetime!

Sarah Franklin is Professor of Anthropology of Science at Lancaster University. In addition to numerous articles and chapters on cloning and reproductive technology, she is the author of *Embodied Progress: a cultural account of assisted* *conception* (1997) and co-author of *Technologies of Procreation: kinship in the age of assisted conception* (1999) and *Global Nature, Global Culture* (2000). Her co-edited anthologies include *Reproducing Reproduction: kinship, power and technological innovation* (1998) and *Relative Values: reconfiguring kinship studies* (2001). She is currently completing a book about cloning entitled *Dolly Mixtures*.

Christian Gamborg has a PhD from the Royal Veterinary and Agricultural University and is a research scientist at the Danish Forest and Landscape Research Institute and at the Centre for Bioethics and Risk Assessment. His research interests include ethics, sustainability and biodiversity in relation to land use, forest and natural resource management.

John Harris is Sir David Alliance Professor of Bioethics at the Institute of Medicine, Law and Bioethics, University of Manchester. He is a member of the United Kingdom Human Genetics Commission and of the Ethics Committee of the British Medical Association. He was one of the founder directors of the International Association of Bioethics and a founder member of the board of the journal *Bioethics* and a member of the editorial board of the *Journal of Medical Ethics* and many other journals.

David King is Coordinator of Human Genetics Alert, a watchdog group focusing on ethical and social issues raised by human genetics. He was formerly editor of *GenEthics News* and Director of the Genetics Forum. He has a PhD in molecular biology from Edinburgh University and a BA from Christ's College, Cambridge. He is a member of the Ethics Group of the North Cumbria Community Genetics Project. He has written for many publications and is a regular contributor to TV and radio current affairs programmes on genetics.

Gill Langley gained her PhD in natural sciences at Cambridge University and is a long-standing animal rights advocate. She works as scientific adviser to the Dr Hadwen Trust for Humane Research, a charity which funds non-animal medical research, and has lectured and published widely. She is also a freelance consultant for anti-vivisection and animal protection organisations in Europe and the USA.

Ralph Levinson is a science educationalist whose main interests are in teacher education, teaching socio-scientific issues and the public understanding of science. He is the author of *Valuable Lessons*, a report commissioned by the Wellcome Trust on the teaching of controversial issues in schools. He has given numerous talks and seminars in the UK, Europe and Brazil. After ten years teaching in London schools and writing curricular materials, he wrote the science line of the Open University PGCE. He has been at the Institute of Education since 1998.

Mark Matfield trained and worked as a medical research scientist in the UK and USA. Since 1988 he has been Executive Director of the Research Defence Society, the main organisation in the UK representing the scientific community in the public and political debate about the use of animals in medical research and testing. He has written and lectured widely on the public understanding of, and public attitudes to, animal experimentation.

Michael J. Reiss is Professor of Science Education at the Institute of Education, University of London, and a priest in the Church of England. He researches and lectures widely in bioethics and science education. He has been chair of EuropaBio's Advisory Group on Ethics and a specialist adviser to the House of Lords on the use of animals. He has provided advice and consultancy for a number of biotechnology and pharmaceutical companies and is a member of the ethics committee of a major infertility clinic.

Peter Sandøe was educated at the University of Copenhagen and at the University of Oxford. From 1992 to 1997 he was Head of the Bioethics Research Group at the University of Copenhagen. He is now Research Professor in Bioethics at the Royal Veterinary and Agricultural University in Copenhagen and director of a newly established interdisciplinary Centre for Bioethics and Risk Assessment. Since 1992 he has served as Chairman of the Danish Ethical Council for Animals and been president of the European Society for Agricultural and Food Ethics.

Marilyn Strathern gained her PhD at Cambridge University and has undertaken fieldwork in Papua New Guinea. Currently Professor of Social Anthropology at the University of Cambridge and Mistress of Girton College, she sits on the Nuffield Council of Bioethics. A fellow of the British Academy, and Foreign Hon. Member of the American Academy of Arts & Sciences, she was recently presidential Chair of the European Association of Social Anthropologists. Ethnographic investigations in gender relations (*Women in Between*, 1972) and kinship (*Kindship at the Core*, 1981) led to a critical appraisal of ongoing models of Melanesian societies (*The Gender of the Gift*, 1988), and to some extent of consumer society in Britain (*After Nature*, 1992). The debates around legislation following the Warnock Report stimulated her interest in reproductive technologies and a collaborative research project (1990–91) examining some of the issues in the context of kinship was published as *Technologies of Procreation* (1993). The recently edited collection *Audit Cultures* (2000) touches on the institutionalisation of good practice.

Juliet Tizzard is Director of Progress Educational Trust, a charity set up to promote the benefits of reproductive and genetic science. She is also editor-in-chief of BioNews.org.uk, a web-based news and comment service, also on reproductive and genetic science. A graduate of King's College London's MA in Medical Law and Ethics, Juliet has written on a range of bioethical issues.

Jon Turney lectures in science communication in the Department of Science and Technology Studies at University College London. He has a particular interest in public understanding of the life sciences. He is the author of *Frankenstein's Footsteps: Science, Genetics and Popular Culture* (Yale, 1998), and editor of the Icon Books popular history series *Revolutions in Science*.

Ian Wilmut is the leader of the team which produced Dolly, the first animal to develop after nuclear transfer from an adult cell. The objectives of his research group are to understand mechanisms which regulate early embryo development and to use that knowledge to establish methods for the multiplication and genetic modification of animals.

Part I
Ethics and education

1   Issues and scenarios

Ralph Levinson and Michael J. Reiss

Rationale

The publication of the first draft of the Human Genome Project has been hailed as a revolution surpassing the landing on the moon, and there is little doubt that many of the most pressing concerns in science are in biomedicine and associated reproductive technologies. The new biotechnologies raise huge ethical dilemmas that concern us all and the issues are being played out in the media, not least the tabloid press. Young people too are talking about complex ethical issues, such as GM foods, animal rights and cloning, and bringing their views to bear in the classroom. But are they merely arguing about popular misconceptions and myths that they hear through various media? How informed are we all about the scientific, ethical and social consequences that will affect most of us? Education must have a role. But how can teachers become sufficiently informed about the issues that surround such rapidly advancing technologies, where the legal and ethical implications are changing daily and testing even experts in the field?

Most of us are under-prepared for the challenges to our ethical and legal system that these technologies pose. The main voices heard are those of generic journalists, followed by the relatively few scientifically trained journalists, followed a long way behind by scientists and ethicists working in the field. The voices of those likely to be most affected – disabled people, ethnic groups, women, people with genetic conditions, gays and lesbians, those unable to have children – are all too rarely heard. If we are to understand and talk rationally about the ethical issues we need to know the views of people who have worked in these fields and thought deeply about these issues, the grounds for their beliefs and the controversies generated by differences in points of view. There is little unanimity here, which adds to the complexity.

This book develops informed conversations between ethicists, scientists and those who have a stake in these new technologies. These conversations come from articulate people who are passionately and intellectually committed to well-thought-out perspectives. The book is aimed at teachers and others who want an insight into the ethical and social arguments and the opinions of a wide spectrum of people.

What is bioethics?

For many centuries ethics has concerned itself with such questions as 'What is right and what is wrong?', 'Should we always tell the truth?', 'When, if ever, is it right to kill someone?' and 'Is it fair that some people can buy better education for their children?'. Over the last few decades moral philosophers and others have realised how such questions generally assume that only human beings are objects of moral concern. With the rise in the environmental movement, the growing concern for the well-being of animals and the increasing importance of new biotechnologies, whether in medicine or agriculture, the term 'bioethics' is increasingly being used.

No single definition of the word 'bioethics' can be given. In the USA, for example, the term is still sometimes used as a synonym for 'medical ethics' (e.g. Shannon, 1993). In most countries, though, it is used (e.g. Gillon, 1998) to encompass all the questions about ethics in biology and medicine, including those that could not have been asked thirty years ago. It is in this latter, wider sense that the word is used in this book.

More important, perhaps, than agreement about how the word bioethics is used is an understanding of how bioethics is done. We hope that anyone reading the contributions in this volume will realise how wide are the demands on anyone who hopes to write well about bioethics. The science is important; an understanding of how ethical arguments can be constructed is important; an appreciation of the law is often needed; and an understanding of psychology and sociology helps too.

An example of how bioethical argument is constructed is provided by the recent debates over stem cell research. A brief discussion of this question also has the merit of indicating the role that religious arguments can play in bioethics. This is an important issue as there are some who would rather that religious views played no role in ethical thought, while there are others who believe that ethics is fundamentally underpinned by religion.

Doing bioethics – the example of the controversy over stem cell research

After a human egg and sperm join in fertilisation, an embryo begins to develop. By five days after conception, a hollow ball of cells has formed. The outer cell layer gives rise to the placenta. The inner 50 or so cells are known as pluripotent embryonic stem cells and go on to form the tissues of the developing embryo. Each of these embryonic stem cells can give rise to most cell types that make up an adult human body.

As the embryo continues to develop, its cells become increasingly differentiated. Most of them lose the capacity to develop into a wide range of cells. Instead they become specialised, functioning as a red blood cell, one of the cell types in bone, or whatever. However, even in adults some cells naturally retain a certain capacity to give rise to a variety of different cell types. For example, blood stem cells, located in bone marrow, can develop into red blood cells, platelets and the various sorts of white blood cells.

One way in which stem cells might be used is by what is generally referred to as therapeutic cloning. In therapeutic cloning a patient needing a transplant would have one of their ordinary cells removed – this could simply be a cell from the base of a hair or any other suitable tissue. This cell, or its nucleus, would then be fused with an egg cell from which the nucleus had been removed.

This resulting cell would then be stimulated to divide in the same way that the cell that gave rise to Dolly the cloned sheep was (see Chapter 4). If all went to plan, stem cells could then be isolated from this developing embryo and encouraged to develop into tissues. It is hoped that these tissues could then be used for transplantation. For example, a person with Parkinson's disease might receive a transplant of neural cells.

The principal ethical argument in favour of therapeutic human cloning is easily stated. It is that this technology stands a good chance of reducing human suffering and enhancing happiness. Indeed, it has been estimated that over one-third of the people in the United States are affected by diseases that may be helped by stem cell research (Perry, 2000). It may be that such benefits will be found to result from other technologies, for example through using stem cells derived from adults or from umbilical cords. However, most scientists believe that adult stem cells are likely to be less valuable for research and in developing new treatments than are the pluripotent stem cells that can only be derived from human embryos (e.g. Royal Society, 2000).

The main ethical arguments against therapeutic human cloning centre on questions to do with the status of the human embryo. Different people see the status of the human embryo very differently. As the official

UK government committee set up to report on human stem cell research put it:

> A significant body of opinion holds that, as a moral principle, the use of any embryo for research purposes is unethical and unacceptable on the grounds that an embryo should be accorded full human status from the moment of its creation. At the other end of the spectrum, some argue that the embryo requires and deserves no particular moral attention whatsoever. Others accept the special status of an embryo as a potential human being, yet argue that the respect due to the embryo increases as it develops and that this respect, in the early stages in particular, may properly be weighed against the potential benefits arising from the proposed research.
>
> (Department of Health, 2000, para. 17 of the Executive Summary)

The history in the twentieth century – and not just in Nazi Germany (e.g. Hornblum, 1998) – of what are now regarded as unacceptable instances of experimentation on human subjects means that the current very considerable hesitation about research on human embryos is not just understandable but, surely, to be welcomed. For many people the central question is the extent to which a human embryo with a relatively small number of cells that is, undoubtedly, completely incapable of feeling or thinking anything has some or all of the rights or respect due to the human newborn baby or adult into which it has the potential to develop.

Religious traditions hold varying views about the embryo's value and status (House of Lords, 2002; Wertz, 2002) Most of the existing writing pertinent to stem cell research is of Jewish or Christian origin. Jewish views hold that a foetus outside the mother's body does not have the same value as a fetus within her body. Traditionally a foetus was 'water' for the first 40 days. Most Jewish commentators speak of a mandate to heal and some would allow the creation of embryos in a Petri dish for research. In evidence submitted to the House of Lords the Court of the Chief Rabbi stated:

> In Jewish law neither the foetus nor the pre-implanted embryo is a person; it is, however, human life and must be accorded the respect due to human life. Personhood, with its attendant rights and responsibilities begins at birth. Prior to birth, we have duties to both the embryo and the foetus, but these may, in certain circumstances, be overridden by other duties, namely those we owe to persons.
>
> (House of Lords, 2002, p. 23)

According to Thomas Aquinas (following Aristotle and St Augustine), rational souls entered males at 40 days and females at 90 days; before that embryos had only a vegetative life force. No one would nowadays defend this gender difference but Aquinas' view highlights an ongoing area of debate within the Christian churches: whether the embryo should be accorded, or has, full human status from the moment of conception or, in mainstream contemporary Protestant thinking, grows into personhood.

Most of the ethical questions concerning the status of the embryo have long been examined in the context of abortion (Reiss, 2002). Given that a widespread consensus on the moral status of the human embryo not only does not exist – and has probably not existed over many centuries of debate – but seems extremely unlikely to exist in the near future, the role of ethicists may be not so much to attempt to produce a definitive answer to the question of the status of the human embryo in the very early developmental stages at which therapeutic human cloning would take place, but more to help clarify arguments and indicate the implications of particular approaches.

To be or not to be

Developments in technology, as indicated, have led to ever more pressing questions about who should be born and who should not be born. Decisions of this nature are invariably complex and painful but it is possible to take seemingly contradictory viewpoints at the same time. When asked about animal experimentation, for example, people may express the view that they feel concerned about the use of such animals in medical experiments but assert that they have benefited from treatment that has involved medicines first tested on animals. We might be opposed to genetic selection of embryos for life-threatening conditions but empathise with parents who want to use this procedure. In so many instances the way we respond to a dilemma in the context of society as a whole can contradict a decision we might come to at a personal level.

'Informed decision-making' is a phrase frequently used in educational circles but we should recognise that the more we are informed about something the more difficult it can be to make a particular decision. Once we consider extra factors, what seems like a simple decision can become enormously difficult. A mother, for example, may agree to be tested in early pregnancy to check if the embryo tests positive for a disabling genetic condition. Of itself, this appears innocuous. But how would the mother's decision be influenced if she was told that the test carries a risk that might result in a miscarriage? And what would she do if informed that the medicines and technology becoming available can, in any case, ameliorate this genetic condition? When the effect on family and siblings are considered, the decision may be even more difficult. But these consequences and the weighing of risks against benefits are not the only ways of thinking about these concerns. If you believe abortion is wrong no matter what the outcome of the test, then why have the test in the first place? Well, it may help you prepare for the baby if she does have a genetic condition but why take the chance if the test might be in error? Or if you know the test is highly accurate and very rarely results in a miscarriage would you be more likely to try it?

In Chapter 9 Marilyn Strathern discusses the ways meanings have changed in relation to the term surrogacy. Developments in the Human Genome Project also have significant implications for language use. For some, the genetic code is analogous to information on a disc that can be cut and spliced to correct harmful genes (Ridley, 1999). Identify the villain gene, correct it and disabling conditions can be eradicated. The danger, as perceived by others, is that for disabling genetic conditions the gene becomes the focus of attention rather than the individual, community or society more generally. Very few genetic conditions result in a straightforward expression of genotype to disease. Evelyn Fox Keller has written about the problematic 'glow of the geneticists' spotlight . . . [which allows] neither time nor space in which the rest of the organism, the surplus economy of the soma, could exert its effects' (Fox Keller, 1995, p. xv). How we talk about ourselves and our genes can have an impact on the ethical decisions we make. This is why we believe students should have the space to be able to listen to, discuss and engage in bioethical issues in school so that they can gain insights into some of the complexities.

The chapters in this book are designed to generate debate rather than supply consensus and the authors explore issues from diverse and, sometimes, adversarial perspectives. But the authors justify the positions they take and it is this reasoning, involving insights into the emotions, values and feelings that people bring to consideration of ethical dilemmas, that we feel should be the message of this book.

Organisation of the book

We have structured the book into seven parts. The first three chapters make up Part 1. These three chapters (including this one) deal with generic issues. They outline the boundaries of the controversies, examine the nature of ethical debate and discuss issues to do with teaching in this area.

Ethical debate is at the heart of Parts 2 to 7. Each chapter in these sections focuses on current issues where the ethical dilemmas are considerable and arise from developments in technology. Parts 2, 3, 4 and 5 deal with developments in biomedicine. Parts 6 and 7 examine the ethical issues surrounding the treatment of farm animals and the use of animals for medical experiments. Each of Parts 2 to 7 includes contributions from experts coming from very different positions who debate the issues.

In Part 1, Chapter 2 is by Michael Reiss and discusses how we reach ethical conclusions. It looks at the scope of ethics and at how ethical arguments can validly be conducted. In particular, Reiss looks at whether it is sufficient only to look at what the ethical consequences of an action would be or whether certain actions are right or wrong at least to some extent independently of their consequences. Reiss then goes on to examine the more recent contributions that feminist and virtue ethics have made, before discussing the way in which bioethics seeks to take account of the interests of non-humans and of future generations. The chapter concludes that while there is no single way in which ethical debates about bioethics can unambiguously be resolved, that does not mean that all ethical arguments are equally valid. Reiss maintains that ethical conclusions need to be based on reason, to take into account well established ethical principles and to rest, so far as possible, on consensus. Education and debate also play important roles, helping to enable people to clarify their own thinking, express their views and participate in the democratic process.

Chapter 3 by Ralph Levinson discusses why and how bioethics should be taught in secondary schools. Many research studies show how school students perceive science as dealing in certainties, whereas ethics probes the realm of uncertainties. These opposite epistemic positions cause real problems for science teachers in encouraging debate about ethical dilemmas in the science classroom. But science, like ethics, is about probing the truth rather than claiming it and there need not be a problem in promoting consideration of ethical dilemmas, although Levinson does not under-estimate the difficulties. He first discusses the reasons for teaching bioethics, before exploring how an ethical dilemma might be approached through a case study. The central thesis is the need to weigh arguments and to understand the points of view of the parties involved. This should precede rational and sensitive decision-making. It is *how* a decision is made rather than *what* decision is made that, he claims, is core to teaching bioethics.

Part 2 is about cloning, on which reams of newsprint have been expended and which has provoked intense speculation. During the late 1990s Dolly the sheep became synonymous with cloning. Dolly was the first mammal to be created from non-gamete cells of an adult. The cloning of Dolly projected Professor Ian Wilmut, the leader of the team that cloned Dolly, into world-wide fame. Interviewed by Ralph Levinson in Chapter 4, he talks about the reasons for doing work on cloning and why he is fully opposed to the cloning of humans. He elaborates both on the benefits of the technology and the harm that would accrue if the technology is misused. To avoid this misuse there needs to be a broad social consensus and proper regulations in force. Wilmut takes care to distinguish between therapeutic cloning, to which he gives considered support, and reproductive cloning.

In Chapter 5 Rebecca Bennett and John Harris do not consider that the kinds of objections Ian Wilmut has to human cloning should necessarily lead to the prohibition of reproductive cloning. They carefully address a range of ethical arguments against both reproductive cloning and therapeutic cloning (known also as stem cell therapy) and decide that these arguments are not fully substantiated. Sceptical of the 'tendency towards conservatism in the results of public consultations', they argue that they may do more harm in the long run by impeding the benefits of technology. They call instead for a rigorous application of the principles of moral philosophy to these dilemmas.

'Cloning? Yuk!' is the title of Chapter 6, in which David King launches a vigorous attack on the technology of cloning and those interest groups that support it. He maintains we are on a slippery slope, where the reconfiguration of human reproduction is part and parcel of capitalist production and a distortion of our basic human values. Like Ian Wilmut, he objects forcefully to human cloning but he goes well beyond Wilmut in his opposition to the technology and its dehumanising effects. Deriding 'academic bioethics' in its concern for autonomy and political neutrality, King attempts to identify those social and political factors that enlist bioethicists into maintaining the *status quo*.

In Chapter 7 Sarah Franklin explores the origin of the term 'cloning', suggesting that the technique of cloning is neither new nor necessarily controversial. However, like David King, she understands authentic public anxiety about the technology and its possible consequences. She suggests that media speculation may be unnecessarily alarmist but that the challenges posed by cloning will influence public trust towards genomics and definitions of human identity.

Part 3 is about *in vitro* fertilisation (IVF). IVF has been with us for nearly a quarter of a century and has led to the birth of over a million so-called 'test-tube babies' world-wide. Yet, despite its transition from an experimental to a routine medical intervention, it continues to attract almost as much public and media attention as it did in the late 1970s. In Chapter 8 Juliet Tizzard examines a number of the ethical issues connected to IVF. In particular, she looks at whether those individuals who are sometimes referred to as socially infertile should receive IVF. The 'socially infertile' are those who, because of certain life choices they have made, are unable or unwilling to use natural conception to have children. They include certain single women; men or women in same-sex relationships; women who wish to delay motherhood until their forties or fifties and those women who wish to have a child after the menopause.

In Chapter 9 Dame Marilyn Strathern takes a different approach to issues connected to IVF. She uses her background as an anthropologist to examine one very specific issue – namely what is meant by the term 'surrogacy' and who is the surrogate in a surrogacy contract. In surrogacy, one woman carries (during pregnancy) a developing baby who is then handed over to another woman after its birth. Strathern points out that the question as to which of these two women is 'the surrogate' is now answered differently compared to how it was answered in the early days of surrogacy in the 1980s. The difference in language tells us something about how people understand relationships – i.e. the relationships between the two women involved as well as between each of them and the baby resulting from IVF. Strathern's chapter reminds us that what society deems ethical is connected with how people understand, indeed construct, reality. Is the woman who carries the baby for the nine months of pregnancy the real mother? Or is the real mother the woman who brings the child up? And how, if at all, does genetic relatedness come into all this?

Part 4 looks at genetic screening. In Chapter 10 Jon Turney explores the basis for testing a population for genetic conditions. He discusses the rationale for screening for a particular genetic condition and then goes on to identify a range of problems that may arise through the screening process. As the subtitle of his chapter rightly notes, screening is a 'mixed blessing'.

Elizabeth Anionwu, in Chapter 11, focuses on the cases of sickle cell anaemia and thalassaemia which mainly, though by no means exclusively, affect ethnic minority groups in the UK. Whilst people can take advantage of the screening process, Anionwu makes the point that this is insufficient if the support structures are not in place to assist those who either have the conditions or are carriers. She goes on to identify good and not-so-good practices and gives reasons for the low status often given to consideration of these conditions. Helpfully, she points to some promising ways forward.

Part 5 considers the possibility of genetically engineering humans. In Chapter 12 Bill Albert begins by addressing a widely held position, namely that gene therapy is simply a medical intervention, akin, for example, to inoculation against polio. However, despite the billions of dollars spent and a decade of hype from the biotech-medical industry, there has been no gene therapy which has worked consistently. Research which underpins gene therapy is continuing to identify more targets for prenatal testing and the only proven way to prevent the vast majority of genetic conditions is abortion following a genetic test or embryo selection as part of IVF. It is likely that this is all that will be available for quite some time, especially if we factor in the comparatively high costs of cure as opposed to testing and termination. Albert concludes that what disables people living with genetic disorders are the societies in which they live, not the disorders themselves.

In Chapter 13 Michael Reiss begins by distinguishing between the two main types of gene therapy and then discusses their scope. He points out that even simple genetic diseases actually result from an interaction between genes and the environment. This is even more the case when we consider traits such as intelligence, beauty, criminality and sexual preference. Reiss argues that the history of cosmetic surgery provides a model for a possible future for gene therapy. The resulting comparison suggests that gene therapy may be exploited and lead to some people seeing themselves as genetically inferior who would not previously have done so. At the same time, it is possible to imagine the day when genetic engineering to boost people's intelligence will be widespread. Indeed, there are circumstances when it can be argued that this would be the right thing to do.

Part 6 examines farm animal welfare. In Chapter 14 Christian Gamborg and Peter Sandøe begin by reviewing the history of animal breeding. They then examine ethical aspects of breeding and biotechnology in farm animals. A distinction needs to be made between the ethical issues raised by animal husbandry – which concern existing animals – and those raised by animal breeding –

which concern potential animals. In animal breeding the relevant question is 'What sort of animals should there be?'. In attempting to answer this question, Gamborg and Sandøe critically examine what is meant by such terms as animal welfare and animal integrity. They suggest that the notion of sustainable farm animal breeding may be a useful one.

In Chapter 15 Joyce D'Silva passionately defends the view that many animals can suffer much as we can. She points out that we might all acknowledge a duty of care towards those animals actually in our care – such as pets – but asks whether we also have a duty of care for the animals we end up eating or wearing. She cites instance after instance where modern breeding resulted in farm animals that are in pain or unable to behave naturally. Looking towards the future, she fears that the new technologies of genetic engineering and cloning will exacerbate this situation.

Part 7 looks at the arguments for and against the use of animals in medical experiments. In Chapter 16 Mark Matfield begins by reviewing the history of the use of animals in medical experiments and then addresses the fundamental question as to whether we have the right to use animals in this way. Matfield examines whether non-human animals have rights too or whether other ways of considering the interests they have – for example, by maintaining that they have inherent value – are preferable. He concludes that the balancing of human interests against animal interests is essentially a utilitarian process, seeking the greatest overall good or pleasure.

In Chapter 17 Gill Langley too begins by considering historical aspects. She points out, though, that the fact that animal experiments have figured in many medical developments does not necessarily mean that every advance has benefited from animal experiments or crucially depended on them; equally, it would be incorrect simply to assume that, because animal experiments were so widely used in the last two centuries, they must remain a dominant methodology in the twenty-first century. Langley's principal arguments are, first, that humans do not have the right to use sentient animals for medical experimentation, and, second, that the value to humans of animal experiments is overstated. She then goes on to examine the particular issue of genetic modification, including xenotransplantation. She concludes that science is increasingly being driven by commercial enterprises whose powerful economic interests sometimes conflict with public opinion and policy.

References

Department of Health (2000) *Stem Cell Research: Medical Progress with Responsibility – A Report from the Chief Medical Officer's Expert Group Reviewing the Potential of Developments in Stem Cell Research and Cell Nuclear Replacement to Benefit Human Health*, Department of Health, London.

Fox Keller, E. (1995) *Refiguring Life: Metaphors of Twentieth-Century Biology*, The Wellek Library lecture series, Columbia University Press, New York.

Gillon, R. (1998) Bioethics, overview, in Chadwick, R. (Ed.) *Encyclopedia of Applied Ethics, Volume 1*, Academic Press, New York, pp. 305–17.

Hornblum, A. M. (1998) *Acres of Skin: Human Experiments at Holmesburg Prison – A True Story of Abuse and Exploitation in the Name of Medical Science*, Routledge, New York.

House of Lords (2002) *Stem Cell Research: Report from the Select Committee (HL Paper 83(i))*, Stationery Office, London.

Perry, D. (2000) Patients' voices: the powerful sound in the stem cell debate, *Science*, 287, 1423.

Reiss, M. J. (2002) Ethical dimensions of therapeutic human cloning, *Journal of Biotechnology*, 98, 61–70.

Ridley, M. (1999) *Genome: The Autobiography of a Species in 23 Chapters*, Fourth Estate, London.

Royal Society (2000) *Therapeutic Cloning: A Submission by the Royal Society to the Chief Medical Officer's Expert Group*, The Royal Society, London.

Shannon, T. A. (Ed.) (1993) *Bioethics: Basic Writings on the Key Ethical Questions That Surround the Major, Modern Biological Possibilities and Problems*, 4th Edn, Paulist Press, New Jersey.

Wertz, D. C. (2002) Embryo and stem cell research: views from the USA, *Journal of Commercial Biotechnology*, 8, 200–208.

Biographies

Ralph Levinson is a science educationalist whose main interests are in teacher education, teaching socio-scientific issues and the public understanding of science. He is the author of *Valuable Lessons*, a report commissioned by the Wellcome Trust on the teaching of controversial issues in schools. He has given numerous talks and seminars in the UK, Europe and Brazil. After ten years teaching in London schools and writing curricular materials, he became course chair of the science line of the Open University PGCE. He has been at the Institute of Education since 1998.

Michael J. Reiss is Professor of Science Education at the Institute of Education, University of London, and a priest in the Church of England. He researches and lectures widely in bioethics and science education. He has been chair of EuropaBio's Advisory Group on Ethics and a specialist adviser to the House of Lords on the use of animals. He has provided advice and consultancy for a number of biotechnology and pharmaceutical companies and is a member of the ethics committee of a major infertility clinic.

2   How we reach ethical conclusions

Michael J. Reiss

The scope of ethics

Ethics is the branch of philosophy concerned with how we should decide what is morally wrong and what is morally right. Sometimes the words 'ethics' and 'morals' are used interchangeably. They can, perhaps, be usefully distinguished. We all have to make moral decisions daily on matters great or (more often) small about what is the right thing to do: should I continue to talk to someone for their benefit or make my excuse and leave to do something else? Should I give money to a particular charity appeal? Should I stick absolutely to the speed limit or drive 10% above it if I'm sure it's safe to do so? We may give much thought, little thought or practically no thought at all to such questions. Ethics, though, is a specific discipline which tries to probe the reasoning behind our moral life, particularly by critically examining and analysing the thinking which is or could be used to justify our moral choices and actions in particular situations.

The way ethics is done

Ethics is a branch of knowledge just as other intellectual disciplines, such as science, mathematics and history, are. Ethical thinking is not wholly distinct from thinking in other disciplines but it cannot simply be reduced to them. In particular, ethical conclusions cannot be unambiguously proved in the way that mathematical theorems can. However, this does not mean that all ethical conclusions are equally valid. After all, most philosophers of science would hold that scientific conclusions cannot be unambiguously proved, indeed that they all remain as provisional truths, but this does not mean that my thoughts about the nature of gravity are as valid as Einstein's were. Some conclusions – whether in ethics, science or any other discipline – are more likely to be valid than others.

One can be most confident about the validity and worth of an ethical conclusion if three criteria are met (Reiss, 1999). First, if the arguments that lead to the particular conclusion are convincingly supported by reason. Second, if the arguments are conducted within a well established ethical framework. Third, if a reasonable degree of consensus exists about the validity of the conclusions, arising from a process of genuine debate.

It might be supposed that reason alone is sufficient for one to be confident about an ethical conclusion. However, there are problems in relying on reason alone when thinking ethically. In particular, there still does not exist a single universally accepted framework within which ethical questions can be decided by reason (O'Neill, 1996). Indeed, it is unlikely that such a single universally accepted framework will exist in the foreseeable future, if ever. This is not to say that reason is unnecessary but to acknowledge that reason alone is insufficient. For instance, reason cannot decide between an ethical system which looks only at the consequences of actions and one which considers whether certain actions are right or wrong in themselves, whatever their consequences. Then feminists and others have cautioned against too great an emphasis upon reason. Much of ethics still boils down to views about right and wrong informed more by what seems 'reasonable' than what follows from reasoning.

The insufficiency of reason is a strong argument for conducting debates within well established ethical frameworks, when this is possible. Traditionally, the ethical frameworks most widely accepted in most cultures arose within systems of religious belief. Consider, for example, the questions 'Is it wrong to lie? If so, why?'. There was a time when the great majority of people in many countries would have accepted the answer 'Yes. Because scripture forbids it'. Nowadays, though, not everyone accepts scripture(s) as a source of authority. Another problem, of particular relevance when considering the ethics of biotechnology, is that while the various scriptures of the world's religions have a great deal to say about such issues as theft, killing people and sexual behaviour, they say rather less that can directly be applied to the debates that surround many of today's ethical issues, particularly those involving modern biotechnology. A further issue is that we live in an increasingly plural society. Within any one Western country there is no longer a single shared set of moral values. Instead, there is a degree of moral fragmentation: one cluster of people has this set of ethical views, another has that.

Nevertheless, there is still great value in taking seriously the various traditions – religious and otherwise – that have given rise to ethical conclusions. People do not live their lives in isolation: they grow up within particular moral traditions. Even if we end up departing somewhat from the values we received from our families and those around us as we grew up, none of us derives our moral beliefs from first principles, *ex nihilo*, as it were. In the particular case of moral questions concerning biotechnology and modern medicine, a tradition of ethical reasoning is already beginning to accumulate. For example, most member states of the European Union and many other industrialised countries have official committees or other bodies looking into the ethical issues that surround at least some aspects of biotechnology and contemporary medicine. The tradition of ethical reasoning in this field is nothing like as long established as, for example, the traditions surrounding such age-old questions as war, capital punishment and freedom of speech. Nevertheless, there are the beginnings of such traditions and similar questions are being debated in many countries across the globe.

Given, then, the difficulties in relying solely on either reason or any one particular ethical tradition, we are forced to consider the approach of consensus (Moreno, 1995). It is true that consensus does not solve everything. After all, what does one do when consensus cannot be arrived at? Nor can one be certain that consensus always arrives at the right answer – a consensus once existed that women should not have the vote.

Nonetheless, there are good reasons both in principle and in practice for searching for consensus. Such a consensus should be based on reason and genuine debate and take into account long established practices of ethical reasoning. At the same time, it should be open to criticism, refutation and the possibility of change. Finally, consensus should not be equated with majority voting. Consideration needs to be given to the interests of minorities, particularly if they are especially affected by the outcomes, and to those – such as young children, the mentally infirm and non-humans – unable to participate in the decision-making process. At the same time, it needs to be borne in mind that while a consensus may eventually emerge, there is an interim period when what is more important is simply to engage in valid debate in which the participants respect one another and seek for truth through dialogue (cf. Habermas, 1983).

Is it enough to look at consequences?

The simplest approach to deciding whether an action would be right or wrong is to look at what its consequences would be. No-one supposes that we can ignore the consequences of an action before deciding whether or not it is right. This is obvious when we try to consider, for example, whether imprisonment is the appropriate punishment for certain offences – e.g. robbery. We would need to look at the consequences of imprisonment, as opposed to alternative courses of action such as imposing a fine or requiring community service. Even when complete agreement exists about a moral question, consequences will have been considered.

The deeper question is not whether we need to take consequences into account when making ethical decisions but whether that is all that we need to do. Are there certain actions that are morally required – such as telling the truth – whatever their consequences? Are there other actions – such as betraying confidences – that are wrong irrespective of their consequences? This is about the most fundamental question that can be asked in ethics and it might be expected by anyone who is not an ethicist to expect an unequivocal answer. Unfortunately this is not the case. There still exists genuine academic dispute amongst moral philosophers as to whether or not one needs only to know about the consequences of an action to decide whether it is morally right or wrong.

Those who believe that consequences alone are sufficient to let one decide the rightness or otherwise of a course of action are called consequentialists. The most widespread form of consequentialism is known as utilitarianism. Utilitarianism begins with the assumption that most actions lead to pleasure (typically understood, at least for humans, as happiness) and/or displeasure. In a situation in which there are alternative courses of action, the desirable (i.e. right) action is the one which leads to the greatest net increase in pleasure (i.e. excess of pleasure over displeasure, where displeasure means the opposite of pleasure, that is, hurt, harm or suffering).

Utilitarianism as a significant movement arose in Britain at the end of the eighteenth century with the work of Jeremy Bentham and J. S. Mill. It now exists in various forms. For example, some utilitarians – preference utilitarians – argue for a subjective understanding of pleasure in terms of an individual's own conception of his/her well-being. After all, if I prefer to spend my Saturday evenings re-arranging my cornflake collection, who are you to say that there are other more pleasurable ways in which I could spend my time? What all utilitarians hold in common is the rejection of the view that certain things are right or wrong in themselves, irrespective of their consequences.

Consider the question as to whether or not we should tell the truth. A utilitarian would hesitate to provide an unqualified 'yes' as a universal answer. Indeed, utilitarians have no moral absolutes beyond the maximisation of pleasure principle. Instead, it would probably be necessary for a utilitarian to look in some detail at particular cases and see in each of them whether telling the truth would indeed lead to the greatest net increase in pleasure.

There are two great strengths of utilitarianism. First, it provides a single ethical framework in which, in principle, any moral question may be answered. It doesn't matter whether we are talking about the legalisation of cannabis, the age of consent, the patenting of DNA or the widespread use of genetic screening; a utilitarian perspective exists. Second, utilitarianism takes pleasure and happiness seriously. The general public may sometimes suspect that ethics is all about telling people what not to do. Utilitarians proclaim the positive message that people should simply do what maximises the total amount of pleasure in the world.

However, there are difficulties with utilitarianism as the sole arbiter in ethical decision-making. For one thing, an extreme form of utilitarianism in which every possible course of action would have to be consciously analysed in terms of its countless consequences would quickly bring practically all human activity to a stop. Then there is the question as to how pleasure can be measured. For a start, is pleasure to be equated with well-being, happiness or the fulfilment of choice? And, anyway, what are its units? How can we compare different types of pleasure, for example sexual and aesthetic? Is it always the case that two units of pleasure should outweigh one unit of displeasure? Suppose two people each need a single kidney. Should one person (with two kidneys) be killed so that two may live (each with one kidney)?

Utilitarians claim to provide answers to all such objections (e.g. Singer, 1993). For example, rule-based utilitarianism accepts that the best course of action is often served by following certain rules – such as 'Tell the truth'. Then, a deeper analysis of the kidney example suggests that if society really did allow one person to be killed so that two others could live, many of us might spend so much of our time going around afraid of being hit over the head at any moment that the sum total of human happiness would be less than if we outlawed such practices.

Intrinsic ethical principles

The major alternative to utilitarianism is a form of ethical thinking in which certain actions are considered right and others wrong in themselves, i.e. intrinsically, regardless of the consequences. Consider, for example, the question as to whether a society should introduce capital punishment. A utilitarian would decide whether or not capital punishment was morally right by attempting to quantify the effects it would have on the society. Large amounts of empirical data would need to be collected, comparing societies with capital punishment and those without it with regard to such things as crime rates, the level of fear experienced by people worried about crime and the use to which any money saved by the introduction of capital punishment might be put. On the other hand, someone could argue that, regardless of the consequences of introducing capital punishment, it is simply wrong to take a person's life, whatever the circumstances. Equally, someone could argue that certain crimes, for example first-degree murder, should result in the death penalty – that this simply is the right way to punish such a crime.

There are a number of possible intrinsic ethical principles and because these are normally concerned with rights and obligations of various kinds, this approach to ethics is often labelled 'deontological' (i.e. 'rights discourse'). Perhaps the most important such principles are thought to be those of autonomy and justice.

People act autonomously if they are able to make their own informed decisions and then put them into practice. At a common sense level, the principle of autonomy is why people need to have access to relevant information, for example before consenting to a medical procedure such as an operation.

There has been a strong move towards the notion of increased autonomy in many countries in recent decades. Until recently, for example, most doctors saw their role as simply providing the best medical care for their patients. If a doctor thought, for instance, that a patient would find it upsetting to be told that they had cancer, they generally did not tell them. Nowadays, any doctor withholding such information might find themselves sued. Society increasingly feels that the important decisions should be made not by the doctors but by the patients (or their close relatives in the case of children or adults unable to make their own decisions).

Of course, such autonomy comes at a cost. It takes a doctor time to explain what the various alternative courses of action are – time that could be spent treating other patients. In addition, some doctors feel de-skilled, while some patients would simply rather their doctor made the best decision on their behalf. Overall, though, the movement towards greater patient autonomy seems unlikely to go away in the near future.

Autonomy is not a universal good. Someone can autonomously choose to be totally selfish. If society grants people the right to be autonomous, society may also expect people to act responsibly, taking account of the effects of their autonomous decisions on others.

Autonomy is concerned with an individual's rights. Justice is construed more broadly. Essentially, justice is about fair treatment and the fair distribution of resources or opportunities. Considerable disagreement exists about what precisely counts as fair treatment and a fair distribution of resources. For example, some people accept that an unequal distribution of certain resources (e.g. educational opportunities) may be fair provided certain other criteria are satisfied (e.g. the educational opportunities are purchased with money earned or inherited). At the other extreme, it can be argued that we should all be completely altruistic. However, as Nietzsche pointed out, it is surely impossible to argue that people should (let alone believe that they will) treat absolute strangers as they treat their children or spouses. Perhaps it is rational for us all to be egoists, at least to some extent.

If it is the case that arguments about ethics should be conducted solely within a consequentialist framework, then the issues are considerably simplified. Deciding whether something is right or wrong now reduces to a series of detailed, in depth studies of particular cases. As far as modern medicine and bio-technology are concerned, ethicists still have a role to play but of perhaps greater importance are scientists and others who know about risks and safety, while sociologists, psychologists, policy makers and politicians who know about people's reactions and public opinions also have a significant role.

Much energy can be wasted when utilitarians and deontologists argue. There is little if any common ground on which the argument can take place, though some philosophers argue that there can be no theory of rights and obligations without responsibility for consequences, and no evaluation of consequences without reference to rights and obligations. The safest conclusion is that it is best to look both at the consequences of any proposed course of action and at any relevant intrinsic considerations before reaching an ethical conclusion.

Feminist ethics and virtue ethics

All the above may sound rather rational and calculating, in a pejorative sense. Two movements within moral philosophy have grown in strength recently in partial opposition to this: feminist ethics and virtue ethics.

Feminist ethics is one of the many products of feminism, a movement whose roots go back a long time but which grew in prominence and impact in the second half of the twentieth century, beginning in France and the USA. Chief among the tenets of feminism is the belief that women have been and still are being denied equality with men, both intentionally and unintentionally. This inequality operates both on an individual level (e.g. discrimination in favour of a male candidate over an equally good female candidate for a senior job) and at a societal level (e.g. negligible access to state childcare makes it extremely difficult for women in certain careers to return to full-time work after having a child).

Feminist ethics, in the words of Rosemary Tong, 'is an attempt to revise, reformulate, or rethink those aspects of traditional Western ethics that depreciate or devalue women's moral experience' (Tong, 1998, p. 261). For a start, feminist philosophers fault traditional Western ethics for showing little concern for women's as opposed to men's interests and rights. There has, for example, been a lot more written about when a war is just than about who should care for the elderly.

Then there was the discovery that some of the best known and most widely used scales of moral development (yes, such things do exist) tended to favour men rather than women because the scoring system favoured the rational use of the mind, with the application of impartial, universal rules, over more holistic judgements aimed at preserving significant relationships between people (Gilligan, 1982).

Third, there is the feminist argument that moral philosophers have tended to privilege such 'masculine' traits as autonomy and independence over 'feminine' ones such as caring, striving for community, valuing emotions and accepting the body.

One area in which feminist ethics has made a major contribution in recent years is reproductive medicine. There had been a tendency for mostly male doctors to see any way of treating human infertility as an unquestioned good. Actually, much infertility treatment is physically and emotionally very demanding, particularly on women. A number of feminist authors have also been extremely suspicious about the possibility of the genetic engineering of humans, suspecting that women are being used as guinea pigs or merely to produce 'perfect babies' (e.g. Rowland, 1993).

Virtue ethics holds that what is of central moral significance are the motives and characters of individuals rather than what they actually 'do'. The emphasis is therefore more on those personal traits that are fairly stable over time and which define the moral nature of a person. Think, for example, of the virtues we might desire in someone, whether a friend, an employer or a politician. We might hope that they (and we) would be honest, caring, thoughtful, loyal, humane, truthful, courageous and so on.

Of course, as Aristotle pointed out almost two and a half thousand years ago, any virtue can be taken to excess. Loyalty to one's friends is generally a good thing, but it is better to report your friend to the police if you have reasonable cause to think that he or she is about to murder someone.

In practice, working out precisely what the virtuous thing to do in a situation is virtually impossible. Consider euthanasia. Is it more caring absolutely to forbid euthanasia or to permit it in certain circumstances? And what exactly are the virtues we would wish to see exercised in biotechnology or modern medicine? Despite such difficulties – difficulties which attend every ethical set of principles – there seems little doubt that the world would be a better place if we were all even a bit more virtuous.

Listening to all the voices

Traditionally, ethics has concentrated mainly upon actions that take place between people at one point in time. In recent decades, however, moral philosophy has widened its scope in two important ways. First, intergenerational issues are recognised as being of importance (e.g. Cooper and Palmer, 1995). Secondly, interspecific issues are now increasingly taken into account (e.g. Rachels, 1991). These issues go to the heart of 'Who is my neighbour?'.

Interspecific issues are of obvious importance when considering biotechnology and ecological questions. Put at its starkest, is it sufficient only to consider humans or do other species need also to be taken into account? Consider, for example, the use of new practices (such as growth promoters or embryo transfer) to increase the productivity of farm animals. An increasing number of people feel that the effects of such new practices on the farm animals need to be considered as at least part of the ethical equation before reaching a conclusion. This is not, of course, necessarily to accept that the interests of non-humans are equal to those of humans. While some people do argue that this is the case, others accept that while non-humans have interests these are generally less morally significant than those of humans.

Accepting that interspecific issues need to be considered leads one to ask how. Need we only consider animal suffering? For example, would it be right to produce, whether by conventional breeding or modern biotechnology, a pig unable to detect pain and unresponsive to other pigs (Reiss, 2002)? Such a pig would not be able to suffer and its use might well lead to significant productivity gains: it might, for example, be possible to keep it at very high stocking densities. Someone arguing that such a course of action would be wrong would not be able to argue thus on the grounds of animal suffering. Other criteria would have to be invoked. It might be argued that such a course of action would be disrespectful to pigs or that it would involve treating them only as means to human ends and not, even to a limited extent, as ends in themselves. This example again illustrates the distinction between utilitarian and deontological forms of ethical reasoning, as the issue of pain can be separated from that of rights and obligations in this case.

Intergenerational as well as interspecific considerations may need to be taken into account. Nowadays we are more aware of the possibility that our actions may affect not only those a long way away from us in space (e.g. acid rain produced in one country falling in another) but also those a long way away from us in time (e.g. increasing atmospheric carbon dioxide levels may alter the climate for generations to come). Human nature being what it is, it is all too easy to forget the interests of those a long way away from ourselves. Accordingly, a conscious effort needs to be made to think about the consequences of our actions not only for those alive today and living near us, about whom it is easiest to be most concerned.

Conclusions

There is no single way in which ethical debates about bioethics can unambiguously be resolved. However, that does not mean that all ethical arguments are equally valid. Ethical conclusions need to be based on reason, take into account well established ethical principles and rest, so far as possible, on consensus. Education and debate play an important role, helping to enable people to clarify their own thinking, express their views and participate in the democratic process. As far as biotechnology and modern medicine are concerned, a variety of ethical arguments for and against their deployment can be advanced. Deciding whether or not particular instances of modern biotechnology and biomedical science are acceptable means looking in detail at individual cases. To a large extent, this is what the rest of this book does.

References

Cooper, D. E. and Palmer, J. A. (1995) (Eds) *Just Environments: Intergenerational, International and Interspecies Issues* (Routledge, London).

Gilligan, C. (1982) *In a Different Voice* (Harvard University Press, Cambridge, MA).

Habermas, J. (1983) *Moralbewusstsein und kommunikatives Handeln* (Suhrkamp Verlag, Frankfurt am Main).

Moreno, J. D. (1995) *Deciding Together: Bioethics and Moral Consensus* (Oxford University Press, Oxford).

O'Neill, O. (1996) *Towards Justice and Virtue: A Constructive Account of Practical Reasoning* (Cambridge University Press, Cambridge).

Rachels, J. (1991) *Created from Animals: The Moral Implications of Darwinism* (Oxford University Press, Oxford).

Reiss, M. J. (1999) Bioethics, *Journal of Commercial Biotechnology*, 5, pp. 287–93.

Reiss, M. J. (2002) Introduction to ethics and bioethics, in Bryant, J. A., Baggott-Lavelle, L. M. and Searle, J. F. (Eds) *Bioethics for Scientists* (Wiley Liss, New York), pp. 3–17.

Rowland, R. (1993) *Living Laboratories: Women and Reproductive Technology* (Cedar, London).

Singer, P. (1993) *Practical Ethics*, 2nd edn (Cambridge University Press, Cambridge).

Tong, R. (1998) Feminist ethics, in Chadwick, R. (Ed.) *Encyclopedia of Applied Ethics, Volume 2* (Academic Press, New York).

Further reading

Gilligan, C. (1982) *In a Different Voice* (Harvard University Press, Cambridge, MA).

Moreno, J. D. (1995) *Deciding Together: Bioethics and Moral Consensus* (Oxford University Press, Oxford).

Rachels, J. (1991) *Created from Animals: The Moral Implications of Darwinism* (Oxford University Press, Oxford).

Singer, P. (1993) *Practical Ethics*, 2nd edn (Cambridge University Press, Cambridge).

3　Teaching bioethics to young people

Ralph Levinson

Should we teach bioethics?

At the beginning of this millennium advances in the genetic and reproductive technologies have presented society with many new ethical dilemmas. Should we be allowed to select the sex of a child? Should we clone embryos for spare parts? Does an embryo have rights? Would it be permissible for athletes to undergo gene therapy to enhance performance? Should we allow DNA fingerprinting of all citizens? Might genetic screening raise more problems than it solves?

Formulating public policy and creating the conditions for democratic accountability on these issues presuppose a citizenry that has some grasp of the science and an awareness of the underlying values base. Young people entering medical vocations, the social services and teaching will, in particular, need an appropriate background that enables them to deal with the many ethical, social and legal questions that will arise. It would seem then that the school education in bioethics of an emerging lay and professional citizenry is crucial for providing a forum in which to develop decision-making abilities about these issues.

While there is no doubt that the ethical implications of biological advances reside in both the public and the private domain, there are sound objections to teaching bioethics in schools. In biotechnology things change so fast that teachers cannot possibly have sufficient information to feel confident about teaching and debating the ethics of particular developments in the classroom. The same is true of many other types of public and social policy issues. Is the school curriculum an appropriate site to debate the impact of biotechnology on public policy? Many political decisions are neither explicitly nor implicitly addressed in the school curriculum. Government fiscal policy, the European Union, defence spending and decisions on whether the UK should strengthen diplomatic relations with Iran are matters of importance to all of us but few people could possibly have the time, if indeed they had the inclination, to inform themselves sufficiently on how the government should act in each and every case. We tend to devolve responsibility for this kind of decision-making on to those we most trust who are acting on our behalf or, which is not the same thing, those we vote for in general elections, European elections, local council elections, what you will. People do, of course, form pressure groups or new political groupings when they are not happy with the political options open to them but, for the most part, they do this because of allegiances arising from deeply held value positions or when the circumstances particularly affect them. We tend to become active when we are personally affected or when our values are most put at risk. If we were to attend to all these possibilities in the curriculum, well, schools would run day and night. Some may argue that it is a difficult enough job to create a literate and numerate population with a basic understanding of the natural and material world without going into areas of such demanding complexity.

Some people argue that it is unrealistic to expect science teachers to address moral and ethical aspects of science because science deals with descriptions and explanations of the natural and material worlds, whereas ethics examines how we ought to act given the knowledge we have (Hall, 1999). Science, it is claimed, has nothing to say about the way we should act and behave; equally, ethics has nothing to say about science. The skills and knowledge required to teach ethics are thus distinct from those needed to teach science. We could no more expect a biology teacher to teach ethics than we could expect her to teach music, art or business studies. But the difficulty does not stop there. The issues that I have referred to – cloning, genetic testing and so on – transcend ethics and science. As the contributors to this book make clear, an understanding of their implications depends on the context in which we choose to examine them: the companies and infra-structure that finance the technology, the political context around any innovation (note that GM foods initially barely raised a murmur in the US), people's mores, culture and deeply held beliefs. To address all these surely goes beyond the expertise of the most gifted teacher.

Even if we were supplied with superhuman teachers who could confidently address these issues and have accurate and up-to-date information on tap, they would have precious little time to do it. Science curricula are usually more content-loaded than those in other subjects, and teachers would have to fit in the teaching of bioethics in between all the concepts, skills and procedures that take up the rest of the science curriculum. Add to that marking, meetings, report writing, contributing to school policies, parents' evenings, completing the kinds of documentation that accompany much work in education, keeping up with one's subject and professional development, there would be no time left for the trivial luxuries of sleeping and eating.

It may be helpful at this stage to consider examples of what teaching bioethics in the secondary school might look like. There are, of course, different dilemmas arising from developments in biotechnology. Disputes between scientists about the beneficial or detrimental effects of transgenic crops have been overlaid by suspicion about commercial interests behind the technology, the role of government following on from the BSE fiasco in the UK and differences in policy between the British Medical Association and the Royal Society (Thomas, 2000). A basic understanding of recombinant DNA, pollination and ethics will clearly be insufficient in coming to a decision as to whether the use of GM crops is right or wrong. Nonetheless, as discussed later, it is possible to gain some insight into how decisions of this nature are arrived at and how interest groups influence these decisions. At the very least sensible decision-making will include an awareness of the values base and the factors that constitute a good argument. When complex decisions are looked at from personal perspectives, the ethical issues become clearer even if not easy to resolve (Lewis, 1999).

Imagine now a scenario where a young woman and her partner who wish to have a baby have opted to be genetically tested for sickle cell anaemia because they both come from a high risk group. The test confirms that they are both carriers for the gene in question, meaning that there is a one in four chance that their child will have the condition. What should they do with this information? Should they go ahead and have a baby? Should they stay together and adopt children? Should the woman become pregnant and elect to have an abortion if an amniocentesis indicates the baby will have the condition? Should they separate and eventually find new partners who are not carriers? Who should they tell? (For further information see Chapter 11.)

Young people will be able to identify with this dilemma because it does have a personal impact and they can appreciate the feelings of all those involved. The background biology comes well within the remit of what most, say, 15-year-olds might be expected to know. Between cases like the personal dilemma of testing for sickle cell anaemia and the public policy controversies of GM crops are many issues that students can tackle at different levels.

Introducing a biological concept through an ethical perspective can both enhance interest in, and knowledge of, the biology. At a basic level an understanding of the science precedes the making of an ethical decision. If students wish to discuss the ethics around cloning, it makes sense that they know what cloning involves, what a clone is and what a clone is not. There are a number of misconceptions that students, and many adults, have about these technologies, for example that clones are born the same age as the parent and that 'test-tube babies' are born in test tubes.

What stimulates most interest from students in science is an engagement with contemporary issues (Osborne and Collins, 2000). And none could be more contemporary than developments in biomedicine and biotechnology. Furthermore, a lead has already been provided in those courses – Science, Technology and Society (STS), stimulated in the 1970s by concern about the global effects of science – and resources such as Science and Technology in Society (SATIS), produced in the 1980s, that have already been used to teach aspects of bioethics.

What is involved in teaching bioethics?

All moral philosophers agree that ethical conduct is universalised. In other words, ethical conduct goes beyond self-interest; you cannot be acting ethically if you take only your own interests into account. It is the very antithesis of

'I'm all right, Jack'. This can be encompassed within the principle of equal consideration of interests that gives 'weight in our moral deliberations to the like interests of *all* those affected by our actions' (my italics) (Singer, 1979).

This principle has two particularly useful aspects for classroom teaching. First, is the establishment of a basic moral framework. When considering the interests of people equally, we are not concerned with differences in race, wealth or intelligence because *interests are perceived to be independent of any group identity or affiliation*. Equal consideration of interests does not prescribe equal treatment in all cases. If two people need medical treatment, one being slightly injured and the other seriously injured but capable of recovering, and there are only enough resources to treat one of the injured people, then it would follow from this principle that the more seriously injured person should be treated because the *outcome* would be more equal. The slightly injured person may take a little longer to fully recover but the seriously injured person would suffer considerably less pain and possibly avoid death. Equality is asserted as a basic ethical principle, not as a statement of fact, so discussing differential treatment of people because of who or what they are is both antithetical and irrelevant to this principle.

Secondly, this principle leads to a utilitarian perspective. In its classical form deriving from the philosophy of Bentham and Mill, utilitarianism informed a way of guiding a person's actions that maximised pleaure for all concerned. If we substitute 'interests' for 'pleasure', then what is proposed is that we act to maximise the interests of all those affected by our actions without placing our own interests above those of any other. I will use this principle to discuss a bioethical issue. However, there are of course other legitimate ethical perspectives: a rights-based approach, justice, a principilist view based on religion, communitarianism, feminist ethics. Placing a utilitarian perspective to the fore does not reduce the importance of the other perspectives; it is simply a good place to start and I will later return to these other principles briefly.

When teaching bioethics, it helps to keep the question or dilemma very focused (Lock and Ratcliffe, 1998) and, if possible, to give students the opportunity to talk about how they would act given a particular situation. It is very difficult to run a classroom discussion on, say, the rights and wrongs of 'designer' babies. The discussion can quickly become diverted because there is so much to cover. It is much more effective to start with a situated dilemma.

How are science concepts and procedures used in decision-making? In some contexts the knowledge of science required to understand the dilemma at a basic level may be minimal. As the case becomes more complex, so might the science needed to explain more technical points. The science is often related to what the individual has to understand to make decisions and these often have to be based on evidence which is accurate and well-informed. For pedagogic purposes, the question is when to feed in the science and the level of the science that needs to be understood. To tease out how best to approach the teaching of bioethics we can examine one particular example.

A case study

A couple have a two-year-old boy suffering from beta thalassaemia major. The child is likely to die within a few years unless he responds to new medical treatments or has a blood transfusion from a compatible donor. Both prospects look bleak but there is a new technology, pre-implantation genetic diagnosis (PGD), involving the selection of embryos, that may help to save the child's life. In this particular case, a healthy embryo with a compatible blood group suitable for a bone marrow transplant could be selected as a sibling. Should this procedure be allowed? A first casual glance at the situation might be likely to bring the answer 'yes' but a more detailed analysis would raise serious ethical concerns.

At this point it is worth emphasising the scientific principles. Genetic diseases are caused by genetic mutations. The genes are carried on chromosomes, which are lengths of the molecule DNA found in the nucleus of a cell. Each somatic cell in humans, except for red blood cells, has paired copies of 23 chromosomes. Genes are paired on the chromosomes, and alternative forms of genes coding for particular characteristics, such as eye colour, are known as alleles. In the case of beta thalassaemia major, one of the two alleles coding for one of the proteins that go to make up haemoglobin in the blood is faulty. Normally, people carry two 'healthy' alleles but even when there is a mutation in one of them, the other is unaffected and usually dominant and so the carriers, as they are called, carry the faulty allele but do not have the disease. (There are some exceptions, notably Huntington's disease, where the presence of only one mutated gene results in the manifestation of the disease.) However, if two carriers have a baby there is a one in four chance that the baby will have both mutated genes. (The reason for this can be explained through basic Mendelian genetics.) The disease, whether cystic fibrosis, sickle cell anaemia or one of a number of others, will then result.

A screening process is now in place in some countries, which the regulatory authorities have allowed to be carried out for certain genetic conditions. In the late 1990s technologies became available that allow parents to select an embryo, i.e. a potential baby, with certain characteristics, the main technology being PGD. Briefly, multiple egg production is stimulated by giving the mother-to-be a drug. The eggs are surgically removed from the womb and fertilised *in vitro*. One or more cells are removed from the developing embryo 2 days to 4 days after fertilisation, and these cells are then tested for the genes of certain life-threatening or disabling conditions, such as beta thalassaemia major. Embryos without the allele causing the disabling condition are then re-implanted in the womb. The other embryos are discarded – frozen for further research or destroyed.

From the standpoint of equal consideration of interests, we need to identify the parties most affected. These obviously include the sick child, the parents (convenient to consider them as a unit) and the eventual newborn baby. There are also other parties who may have a stake in the outcome: families in similar situations, the medical profession and society more broadly. Are there competing interests and how should we weigh them up?

We can see that the sick child would gain. His suffering may be considerably reduced, he may be able to live a broadly fulfilling life and he may have the pleasure, perhaps not entirely unalloyed, of a new younger sibling. Even if the treatment does not work, he is no worse off than he was before, assuming that he is at an age where he is unaware of the consequences of failure. Offset against this, however, may be the feeling that his well–being and indeed life are entirely predicated on the existence of his younger sibling.

There are gains, too, for the newborn baby, although these are more problematic. There is, of course, life free from a disabling condition where previously there would have been no existence. But the life was brought about, at least in part, to supply life-saving matching tissue to an older sibling and can be viewed as a means to an end and not entirely as a longed for, unconditionally loved baby. Here again there are gains, though perhaps they are more equivocal in that the child has a life but there is a chance that the child may feel it was born only for the blood it could offer for transfusion purposes.

One of the reasons why this procedure has been thought acceptable is that the blood necessary for transfusion is taken from the umbilical cord of the new-born baby at birth and frozen until it is ready for transfusion into the bone marrow of the sibling. Interventions after birth should not be necessary if all goes well. There would appear to be no problems with this procedure if there was a very high chance of success. But there are points of possible failure at each step of the process. The screening process may not be accurate, *in vitro* fertilisation may not take place, and even when it does, re-implantation in the womb is itself a risky business; although a number of 'healthy' embryos are implanted, there is still a high risk of miscarriage. Implanting multiple embryos will also increase the risk of multiple births with its attendant problems and costs and could increase the chances of litigation by the parents. Finally, the tissue typing and transfusion may not be successful.

Will there be a gain for the parents? They may have a new healthy child who will save the life of their sick child. To offset their gains there is the possibility that the procedure will not work. Then their hopes will have been dashed and the mother will have gone through a difficult and emotionally trying procedure – having had drugs administered to stimulate superovulation and a pregnancy that may result in a miscarriage. Many mothers and potential mothers have miscarriages which cause a lot of distress but the distress in this case will be all the greater given the particular hopes that were placed on the birth.

There have been a few recorded instances to date where the 'healthy' baby produced by PGD was born successfully, but there has not been enough time to see whether the technique has been successful in saving the lives of the older siblings.

Other interest groups

The impact of this procedure will spread well beyond the immediate family. Other families in similar situations will have an interest in the outcome of the procedure and will also have their expectations raised. At present these procedures are not freely available in the UK on the National Health Service. There are then two problems: can we justify raising people's expectations in this way? And if expectations are raised and the procedure is successful, if only in a limited way, will it be only the wealthy who can afford the technology? In some countries, such as the United States where health care is dispensed according to the amounts paid into a health insurance policy, it is clear that availability of these procedures will be differentiated. This raises larger questions of social justice; the implications of this procedure are wide-ranging and rest not only on its success. Will the gain for one family if the procedure is successful be greater than the possible disadvantages for society in general?

Alternatively, the success of the procedure may put strains on the health service, with more people wanting access to PGD. Such access may only come about at the expense of other facilities and there may then be very complex balancing acts to carry out. These, of course, cannot always be predicted but it is an aspect that students ought to note, even if the weighing of possibilities is likely to be beyond the capabilities of any but the 'experts'. Nonetheless, the broader kinds of judgements have to be made by society at large.

Finally, there is a broader metaphysical point, which does come into the framework of equal consideration of interests. The term 'selection' resonates with connotations of eugenics, of selecting those with the right kinds of genes, reinforcing the ideas of superior physical and intellectual characteristics. Some claim that 'aiming for the conception and birth of normal people' need not conflict with the rights of disabled people and the insistence on respecting them as equals (Glover, 2001). How do we take into account the rights of disabled people when, as Bill Albert describes in Chapter 12, their interests are, too often, overridden?

Teaching approaches

There is no one way to teach ethical issues arising from science and the aim of this section is to offer some strategies that may aid learning when discussing bioethics. A lesson of this kind will need a great deal of preparation but once prepared, enacted, evaluated and modified can be used again. The processes engaged in can be used to create other case studies. One model is to start from the dilemma and feed in the science on a need-to-know basis. The preparation will involve taking a case study, articulating the dilemma and anticipating the consequences of a course of action in terms of maximising the interests of those affected. Students should have a grasp of the underpinning science concepts so that they can access more complex knowledge if they need to. Deciding at which level to pitch the case study may be based on what students already know. Now there is such a vast array of resources dedicated to teaching ethical issues, particularly in biomedicine, that it is relatively easy to access the necessary information. A list of resources is given at the end of this chapter.

One of the challenges in teaching bioethics is that the teacher needs to anticipate some of the ethical arguments that students may raise. This does not mean that the teacher has to have a ready answer – there rarely is a ready answer – it is more that students need to be guided in their thinking, so that alternative possibilities can be presented or objections raised. If the teacher has planned a lesson, or series of lessons, around an ethical dilemma, she will feel more confidence in promoting discussion when she can anticipate students' arguments and the students will, in turn, feel more confidence in the teacher. This is very different from being the fount of all knowledge; it is more about being authoritative and prepared. A way of doing this is to present the students with a tabloid newspaper article or a simple narrative outlining the dilemma to be addressed, such as 'Should parents be allowed to choose the sex of their child?' or 'Should we breed pigs for organ transplantation?'. This could be done towards the end of the previous lesson so that students' ideas can be identified beforehand.

Learning bioethics involves, amongst other things, discussion of interests so there need to be opportunities for students to talk, read critically and listen to others. There is unlikely to be complete agreement but students should have the opportunity to communicate their views. It is reasonable to prompt students to justify their viewpoints, perhaps by asking them to explain why one course of action is preferable to another.

In the case of PGD for the treatment of beta thalassaemia major discussed above, there are several interested parties so the class can be divided into groups, with each group considering the interests of one party. Interested parties would include the donor baby, the sick child, the parents, the doctor or medical advisers, a disabled persons' group, and a relatively poor family with a child suffering from beta thalassaemia major. Newspaper cuttings, lists of relevant websites, audiotapes of experiences of interested parties and sections of video can be used to stimulate discussion. A group of students could consider the interests of one of the parties through a list of focused questions, e.g. as the mother of the baby:

- How do you think you will feel when you undergo PGD?
- How are you going to pay for the treatment?
- What are the chances of success?
- What will you do if the procedure does not work?
- Are there any other courses of action open to you?
- Why do you think PGD is preferable to these other courses?
- How do you think you will feel towards your second baby?

Another group considering the interests of the sick child could act as inter-locutors for the first group. As well as presenting the main interests of the sick child they could start off by clarifying the position of, and suggesting counter-arguments to, the first group. Then the roles could be reversed. This gives a focus to the listening group through such questions as: 'Are you saying this . . . ?' and 'But an argument against PGD could be . . .'.

Assembling the necessary elements to construct an argument is an effective way of encouraging students to reason towards a conclusion. An argument can be seen to consist of a claim, a conclusion, evidence that supports the claim and anticipation of evidence that refutes the claim. Students could be supported in doing this through a writing frame (Wellington and Osborne, 2001), as follows:

> There is a lot of discussion about selection of embryos to cure genetic diseases in older siblings
> Some people think this is a good idea because . . .
> Others think it is a good idea because. . . . .
> Further arguments that are in favour are . . .
> But some people think that it is not a good idea because . . .
> Others say . . .
> Further arguments against are . . .
> Having looked at the arguments for and against I think . . .

Completing these writing frames could involve students working as a group to put forward different pieces of evidence in favour and against, or one group could collate evidence for and another group against.

Organising a discussion of this kind in a one-hour lesson is not easy because such a lesson requires students to engage in reflective deliberation and it may take them some time to come up with coherent arguments. There is often a period of seemingly off-task chat, where the group are setting the norms for the conversation and there is likely to be a great deal of changing of minds. Sometimes students say very little because they need time to think. It is wise not to be too ambitious at first but to set limited objectives. Once students begin to acculturate to this kind of discussion, it should make it easier to run next time. Put a time limit of, say, ten minutes on discussion so the students stay focused and there is time for feedback and display.

One of the most common outcomes is a written piece of work. As an impor-tant and desirable skill students should be able to write a discursive argument that incorporates both an understanding of the ethical issues and a knowledge of the science concepts. The writing frame will facilitate this outcome. But there are other ways in which students can gain an understanding of the issue. For example, they could make a display in the science area outlining the dilemma and the viewpoints of the different interested parties. A box could be left out with slips of paper for other students to post any views that they have. Students could make a radio programme (possibly to be broadcast on a local radio station – or, who knows, a national radio station!) in a documentary style where different parties are interviewed, ensuring that reasons for action are based on evidence. The programme could raise questions for its audience. Alternatively, groups of students could make a short video from their own perspectives and these could perhaps be placed on the school's website. An article could be written for the local newspaper or a website could be set up where different parties give their own viewpoints. These could all be used as valuable resources for helping students to develop the skills required to make informed decisions.

The teacher's role

Students sometimes consider an ethical dilemma with deeply held convictions. Great care should be taken that such beliefs, whatever they are, are dealt with sensitively and not held up to ridicule. It needs to be emphasised in the classroom that ideas are being carefully discussed and no student has to accept one view over another. This raises important questions about the role of the teacher when discussing ethical dilemmas because students may look up to the teacher as having authority, and it is quite easy for the teacher to let slip a remark that sways students' viewpoints. Teachers can take various roles such as neutral chair or 'devil's' advocate, each of which has its merits and disadvantages, but whatever role the teacher takes will have implications (Wellington, 1986). A neutral approach may not be convincing to the students because they know the teacher has a point of view and they may select from the teacher's remarks only those parts that they want to hear. Having a balanced approach may not be feasible because the teacher simply cannot address every opinion thrown at her and counterbalance it. Making your opinions known may also court trouble because the teacher might be accused of indoctrination. In England and Wales the Advisory Group on Citizenship advocated a common sense approach so that in certain situations the teacher, when proposing a point of view that students have omitted to consider, might say that there are some viewpoints she would like to share with the class (Department for Education and Employment/Qualifications and Curriculum Authority (DfEE/QCA), 1998). Here the tone of voice and timing can be crucial.

Sometimes a student will find the topic distressing because they have a close relative affected by a condition being discussed. Check any possible sensitivities with the form tutor or head of year. Leave the option open for the student to do something else, for example catch up with some work in the library, or you may decide to avoid the particular issue altogether. Often students are more than willing to talk about their experiences provided there is a supportive atmosphere in the classroom. Students with a relative suffering from cystic fibrosis might want to talk about the treatment provided, or indeed about their own treatments if they are sufferers. One idea used by teachers is the question box, where students can write questions or comments anonymously on a slip of paper, fold the paper and post it in the box. Then the next lesson the teacher can discuss the query in a general way without alluding to specific students.

Some concluding comments

While bioethics is a good vehicle for contextualising and stimulating interest in biology, there may still be some unexpected obstacles when teaching it. When science lessons have been largely content-driven, it can sometimes seem a culture shock to both students and teachers when delving into questions that have no hard answers and where more questions may be raised than solved (Levinson and Turner, 2001). This is why ethical decision-making can often be very complex. But science itself has changed and advanced precisely because its ideas are open to challenge. Science probes the truth but never seeks to claim it. There are now many scientific theories that are so well attested, such as atomic theory, Darwinian evolution and Newtonian mechanics, that it is both time-consuming and pointless to open them to challenge each and every time they are introduced in the classroom. Nonetheless, students ought to know that at some historical point new scientific ideas were very controversial. For example, students could appreciate why people once thought the Earth was flat and at the centre of the universe; why people might have thought fuels lost a burning-promoting substance when they burned rather than combined with oxygen in the air; why people were, and still are, so resistant to accepting that humans have the same ancestors as chimps. Once students begin to have some notion that scientific ideas have often resulted from struggle, grey areas become more acceptable.

In present times there are so many examples where science and technology sit uneasily with society – MMR, BSE, GM foods, Dolly the Sheep, to name but a few – that there is plenty of material to demonstrate to students the importance of considering these matters.

It helps enormously if the teacher is not ploughing a lone furrow in teaching bioethics. Teachers in a department might share their experiences, methods and resources, and the teaching is considerably enhanced where a department structures the curriculum around ethical issues. Whole school approaches will support the teaching of bioethics in three ways: ethos, inter-departmental collaboration and policies related to sex and drugs education.

Learning bioethics effectively, as I have discussed, necessarily involves talk between students and between students and teacher. Individuals should be able to put forward their views in an atmosphere of tolerance such that their views will be listened to with sensitivity and appropriately acknowledged. Some students prefer talking in groups and one-to-one encounters, while others will be quite happy to express their views in whole class discussion. If students have always been used to teacher-led lessons in which they have had very little input, then it will take more time to change the culture of the classroom and one should not expect dramatic changes overnight. Where school councils feature largely in school life, and school policies are open and transparent and invite continuing dialogue between students, staff and governors, then classroom dialogue in science lessons should not be a big transition for students. In many schools that dialogue will already be in place, but it is important to understand those factors that will enhance the teaching of bioethics.

Issues arising from biotechnology and biomedicine are not only addressed in science lessons. They are frequently raised in other subject areas, predominantly English and RE (Levinson and Turner, 2001). Bioethical ideas arise in English when discussing the symbolism of *Frankenstein* and how these issues are contextualised in the media; in Religious Education the ethical arguments are often specifically analysed. This does seem an area where teachers in different subject areas can do some planning together to explore an ethical theme through team-teaching for a day or half a day.

Many schools have policies on sex and drugs education, where students are encouraged to talk about their feelings and moral attitudes. There are elements of a bioethics teaching programme which would have common features with, for example, the technology of reproduction. Thus bioethics may not necessarily be taught discretely in biology but could be taught through a range of subject areas, provided the planning is properly integrated. This again involves whole school thinking about the curriculum.

I have suggested that a utilitarian approach is initially used in the teaching of bioethics. Of course there are other ethical positions. One which is often considered in opposition to utilitarianism is the intrinsic rightness or wrongness of an action. In the case study discussed, such a principled position might be that selection of embryos is simply wrong whatever the possible benefits to the older sibling. There may be good reasons that underpin this position: selection smacks of eugenics, it is the beginning of a slippery slope, we should not be the arbiters over life and death. It is still reasonable, however, to ask someone to justify this position; for example, an effective regulatory mechanism could ensure that the employment of PGD is not abused for purposes other than that of saving life. There are indeed responses to this; good regulations only work as long as government is strong enough to ensure they are enforced. The argument could go on but the point is that students begin to justify their arguments.

Resources

There are some excellent websites from which case studies can be drawn.

The *Guardian* newspaper, the BBC, *Scientific American* and *New Scientist* cover many bioethical issues, which can be found on their websites:
www.guardian.co.uk
www.bbc.co.uk
www.sciam.com
www.newscientist.com

Curriculum resources

The Wellcome Trust (www.wellcome.ac.uk) is the world's biggest charity for biomedical research. It has its own education department, which supports many initiatives on the social and ethical issues of biomedical research. They publish *Labnotes*, which is provided free to all schools and presents accessible scientific information on developments in biomedicine, often with associated activities to explore social and ethical issues.

The National Centre for Biotechnology Education (NCBE; www.ncbe. reading.ac.uk) is based at the University of Reading and produces excellent resources and courses for schools.

The European Initiative for Biotechnology Education (EIBE; www.rdg. ac.uk/EIBE) has produced units of work for schools to stimulate debate on biotechnology issues throughout Europe. These include units on DNA profiling and transgenic plants.

Biological Sciences Curriculum Study (BSCS; www.bscs.org) is a US association developing curriculum materials in biology with some useful resources for studying the social and ethical applications of the Human Genome Project.

Y-touring (www.ytouring.org.uk) is a travelling theatre company whose productions deal mainly with medical, biomedical and biotechnological issues. They perform in schools and other venues. As well as their productions, there are excellent educational resources discussing the science and ethics underlying the themes explored, with advice on running activities in the classroom.

The Genetics Science Learning Center (GSLC; gslc.genetics.utah.edu) is supported by the University of Utah and the Utah Museum of Natural History and has some good resources on genetics in society for primary and secondary school teachers and students.

Useful sources from government, independent and watchdog groups

The Human Fertilisation and Embryology Authority (HFEA; www.hfea. gov.uk) is a statutory UK body which regulates and licenses all research on human embryos. It is a useful source of up-to-date news on developments in biomedicine and their ethical implications.

The Nuffield Council on Bioethics (www.nuffieldbioethics.org) is an independent body. One of its missions is to stimulate public debate on bioethics. It produces a number of reports, such as 'Stem Cell Therapy: Ethical Issues', which will be a good reference source for the teacher. All of its reports can be downloaded from its website.

The Human Genetics Commission (www.hgc.gov.uk) is an advisory body to the government on the social and ethical aspects of human genetics. It provides up-to-date information and public policy consultation documents.

Human Genetics Alert (www.hgalert.org) is an independent watchdog with a critical attitude towards developments in genetics. It provides a press clipping service and critiques of policy which may not always appear in the mainstream press.

References

DfEE/QCA (1998) *Education for Citizenship and the Teaching of Democracy in Schools.*

DfES/QCA (1999) *Science: The National Curriculum for England.*

Glover, J. (2001) Future people, disability and screening, in Harris, J. (ed.) *Bioethics* (Oxford University Press, Oxford).

Hall, E. (1999) Science education and social responsibility, *School Science Review* 81 (295) pp. 14–16.

Levinson, R. and Turner, S. (2001) *Valuable Lessons* (The Wellcome Trust).

Lewis, J. (1999) Genetics, in Reiss, M. (ed.) *Teaching Secondary Biology* (John Murray, London).

Lock, R. and Ratcliffe, M. (1998) Learning about social and ethical applications of science, in Ratcliffe, M. (ed.) *ASE Guide to Secondary Science Education* (The Association for Science Education, Hatfield).

Osborne, J. and Collins, S. (2000) *Students' and Parents' Views of the School Science Curriculum* (King's College, London).

Singer, P. (1979) *Practical Ethics* (Cambridge University Press, Cambridge).

Thomas, J. (2000) Using current controversies in the classroom: opportunities and concerns, *Melbourne Studies in Education*, 41 (2) pp. 133–44.

Wellington, J. (1986) *Controversial Issues in the Curriculum* (Basil Blackwell, Oxford).

Wellington, J. and Osborne, J. (2001) *Language and Literacy in Science Education* (Open University Press, Buckingham).

Part II
Cloning

4   Interview between
Professor Ian Wilmut and
Ralph Levinson

Ian Wilmut

This interview took place at the Roslin Institute on 6 March 2002.

RL In terms of Dolly, what precisely is meant by cloning?

IW Clones are genetically identical animals, which have been produced by taking the nucleus from one cell, a somatic cell, and putting it into an unfertilised egg from which you've removed all the chromosomal material. In practice this means that these animals will have the same chromosomes as the original, but they would differ in the cytoplasmic components of the embryo, including the mitochondria, and they'll almost certainly be carried by a different mother and so be subjected to different effects in the uterus. So they will be very similar; they'll be more similar than any other relative except a genetically identical twin born naturally at the same time.

RL What has been the scientific impact of your work on Dolly?

IW I think the biggest impact is actually in the way that people think. What happens during reproduction is that the single cell of an embryo divides many times and then the cells begin to change to form all the different tissues that make up an adult: the skin, the muscle, reproductive organs; all of the different special tissues. Almost all of those cells have the same genetic information, and yet they function very differently. The understanding had been that these different tissues arose because of progressively more complex and more rigidly fixed differences in the functioning of the genetic information. Until Dolly was born, people had believed that those changes were so fixed that it was not possible to reverse them. By doing the nuclear transfer with our new method we showed that's not true; that you take the genetic information, put it into an egg and sometimes it will then become a new adult.

People are also showing that you can take cells from some adult tissues which are called stem cells because they retain the ability to divide many times and perhaps to form different tissues. These stem cell populations are usually named after the tissue from which they've been derived, so there are neural stem cells, for example, from the central nervous system. Again people had imagined that if you took a cell from a particular tissue, it would only be able to form other cells from that tissue, and there's beginning to be some evidence that's not true either. If you put the cells in a different environment, sometimes they are able to form other tissues. Although I intensely dislike the word 'plasticity', nonetheless it is used to describe this phenomenon – developmental plasticity – implying that the mechanisms that control what a cell does are much less rigidly fixed than we had thought. This is stimulating a huge amount of research to discover just what changes can be made and will have an enormous impact particularly on the development of new treatments for diseases associated with damage to cells that are not repaired or replaced.

RL What are the technological implications?

IW I suppose that there are slightly different uses I have in mind. Now that people have begun to master the technique of doing nuclear transfer in the mouse, an enormous amount of research will be done to understand the basic mechanisms using the mouse. In some species, for example the pig, there will be medical applications, using organs from pigs for transfer into human patients. The reason why that becomes possible through cloning is that we can introduce genetic changes into animals at the same time as cloning them. The way in which this is achieved is by growing the cells from which you are going to produce the animal in the lab for a long time and making precise changes in the genetic information in those cells before they're then used in the nuclear transfer process. There are now cloned pigs in at least two laboratories in North America which have got precise genetic changes introduced into them with a view to making tissues from such pigs suitable for transfer into human patients. In the longer run, it's possible that these sorts of applications will be used in agriculture to make copies of particularly productive, healthy animals. At the present time there are lots of reasons why that's inappropriate; it would be far too expensive; there are lots of welfare implications; but when it becomes a very reliable procedure, I think that will happen on a small scale at least.

RL Have farm animals lost their dignity because they now can be made to be genetically uniform?

IW If the situation you described came about, then I think there would be an ethical concern. I'm not certain that it would come about. I think that there would be some differences between the animals. That's been illustrated recently by the information about the cat where you could see differences in coat colour pattern, even though it is genetically identical to the original. There will be small differences in the appearances of the animals. And I think there will tend to be even bigger differences in personality, because personality is likely to be even less closely controlled than the actual appearance of animals. So I think it remains to be seen what happens, unless you have, let's say, a group of genetically identical dairy cows, people may find they were being treated in a somewhat impersonal way. But it's not certain that that would happen.

RL You just mentioned the cat. A kitten was recently produced at a university in Texas where a private company funded the technology. Isn't this an indication of the drive for profit to make cloned pets and the realisation of people's worst fears about cloning?

IW Yes. I think that there is an underlying motivation in this research with companion animals to have another copy of the same animal, to have the same animal. In some circumstances where the animal has been killed it's to have the original animal back. And I guess I too have slightly conflicting concerns about this in that I don't think it's going to work for the reasons that we've discussed. The animals will probably have different personalities, and it would be likely that a major part of the owner's response to the animal was in personality rather than just in appearance. I think there could be some disappointment. It will be interesting to see exactly what does happen. As far as the commercial exploitation is concerned, isn't it inevitable that if you have a technique which is developed, whether it's making a new type of tape recorder or a new cloth for clothes or a new food, it is going to be provided for customers by companies? That is the sort of society that we have. I can't imagine how this sort of technology could be developed for that particular application, anyway, without there being a commercial involvement.

RL. What ethical approaches do you think should govern the way we use farm animals for scientific research?

IW Well the structure which has formalised here, which I think the people in the group here at Roslin are comfortable working with, is that you have to make a cost–benefit analysis in thinking of research with animals. You have to have a clear idea of the question that you want to answer for the information that you hope to gain by doing an experiment with an animal, and you should only do an experiment if you're expecting to make a significant advance to get significant new understanding. Contrasted with that has to be some thought as to what suffering is involved for the animals in the experimentation. Now, I don't see how you can make a precise measurement, these are not things you can put upon a balance, but I think you have to use your own conscience as well as adhering to the formal structures which operate within and without the institute. You have to make some judgement as to whether you think that the distress you're going to cause the animals is justified by the increased knowledge that you hope to get. Personally, I think that the main effect of the regulatory structures is actually to make people think for themselves. There is a formal structure but the most important thing is to get the people involved in the experimentation to think: 'Is this a really important experiment?', 'Are we doing everything we can to minimise the suffering for the animals?', 'Is it an effectively designed experiment so that as far as we can tell we're very likely to get a clear conclusion?'

We do, formally, have to demonstrate our designs, our ideas, our expectations, to an ethics committee within the institute, as well as to the national regulatory authority which is run by the Home Office and supervises all animal experimentation. Provided that there is a real hope of getting new knowledge, then I think that it is acceptable to do experimentation with animals. I'm quite confident that I've had the benefit of medical treatments that were first assessed and developed with animals. Clearly by my age I've had the advantage of treatment with a great variety of different antibiotics and three different surgeries. If you take proper care to balance the suffering with the knowledge, it is a good thing to do and something that we should continue to do.

RL There have been some concerns about Dolly's arthritis recently. How is Dolly?

IW Well I don't see her every day, but at the present time she is well. As far as we can see she has very little discomfort because of the effects of the anti-inflammatory drugs that she's been given. And so we continue to study her. But just to use this as an example, if it were to happen that her arthritis became more severe so that it was clear that she was in some pain, and if we found that we couldn't ameliorate that, then of course we would be under both a moral obligation and a legal obligation to put her out of her distress and to euthanise her. Fortunately, at the present time that isn't the case.

RL The title of the book that you wrote with Colin Tudge and Keith Campbell is the *The Second Creation*. I wonder if the title of that book might be playing into the hands of those who accuse you of playing God.

IW As I'm sure you realise, book titles are often chosen by publishers rather than by the authors and it took me a while to become accustomed to it. I think it is true, right from the very beginning, that the whole idea of that book was to get people to think. And I think this was expressed quite clearly in the introduction that Colin wrote. We believe very strongly that the scientist, the companies, the clinicians or the patients should not make the judgements as to which techniques should be used. It's much better if they're made as a social judgement because the immediate issues do not distract the people. That was our objective in writing that book. We wanted people to think about the things that will come at some time in the future because it's much easier to think about them a little ahead of time rather than be faced with them at a time when people want to use new treatments.

RL At the time when you were cloning Dolly you must have been aware of the implications. And yet because of the nature of the work, and the way in which scientists work, there isn't the time to have a broader social discussion about this until the deed is done.

IW You raise a very important issue, which is how and when should society become involved in making judgements about science, and I think it's a mistake to think that it's effective to manage science at the stage of the research. And there are two reasons for this: one is that you cannot tell the outcome of science and the second is that you cannot accurately predict the uses of science. Let me illustrate with a couple of examples. We set out to clone from embryo cells with a view to being able to make genetic changes in animals. I suspect any supervisory authority would have said 'yes, that's fine', unaware of the fact that what was going to happen was that cloning was going to be far more powerful than we had imagined, in other words we would be able to clone adults. There are many examples, of course, but perhaps the best known is the prediction by the computer engineer of the late 1940s, I guess, who said that he couldn't imagine the need for more than five computers in the world, ever. Now at that time, to do the man justice, the computers would have been almost the size of a small house. Most houses these days would actually have five computers in them. What you have to do is to research ambitiously and then think cautiously about how you're going to use the technique.

RL You've made your position against human cloning very clear. The concerns that I've identified that you have are with the physical risk of human cloning, and second with the psychological damage to the child. Are there any other factors beyond these which you would bring to bear on human cloning?

IW No. Cloning is a very inefficient process, with an unusually high incidence of late abortions, the birth of dead animals, and, worse, the birth of animals that survive but are abnormal. There's every reason to think that if people did try to clone humans, that's exactly what the outcome would be in the human, or any other species. It's naïve to think that at the present time you could look at the embryos that you produce and select out those that are going to be the healthy offspring. That's why I believe anybody who actually has experience of cloning thinks that it would be grossly irresponsible to think of trying to produce a person at the present time.

RL Let's suppose that over the course of the next ten or twenty years those risks are rapidly decreased. One could argue that if a child is brought up with love and given a careful parent, it doesn't matter how it's generated. Would your objections to cloning then go?

IW Let's reiterate what would happen. You would have a child who would be more similar to the original than any other person except a genetically identical twin born at the same time. Let's consider the example of using this as a way of overcoming infertility and producing a genetically identical copy of one of the parents. Interestingly, it's usually the man who anticipates that he will be copied. I'm sure that's not chance. You have to ask people to consider the relationships that would be created within that family. And I usually do it by describing my own family and then saying, what would happen if there was somebody in it who was twenty years younger, a genetically identical copy of me? You can ask people, would you wish to be a genetically identical copy of your parent? Those who are parents, do you really think that you would treat a child who was a genetically identical twin to you the same way you would treat a child born by natural means? The partner in this hypothetical case: how will she respond to the person as he grows up, who becomes like their partner at the time when their relationship formed? Expectations would be imposed on the child to a far greater extent than normal; not just from other family members but also from school teachers, neighbours, friends, relatives and so on. That makes me think it might not be much fun to be a clone.

RL But IVF was looked upon askance twenty odd years ago. If the cultural stigma of cloning softened, it might become an acceptable thing for people to do.

IW But I think they're different. The child produced by IVF is just like a child produced normally, except the sperm is delivered in a different way, which is less fun. Let's try thinking of specific cases. I imagine that David Beckham's son Brooklyn will inevitably face expectations of being a footballer. If he were a genetically identical copy of David Beckham, it would surely be even worse. A daughter would be expected to be like his wife. I don't see how you can get around that. I'm not clear how long those things would last; I'm not quite clear how heavy the pressure would be, even if it was only, 'well you're absolutely not like your father'. That sort of comment. But that's the only cause of my anxiety because I think that there would be different relationships. That's what worries me.

RL More and more countries are calling for a world-wide moratorium on human cloning. Do you think they're justified?

IW Well for safety grounds I'm sure it's very important. The only reason I hesitate to call for a global moratorium is because the most important thing is to *have* a moratorium, and whether it comes from a whole range of independent countries saying we're not going to let this happen, or whether we wait until everybody's prepared to say it shouldn't happen, it's just really a practical choice as far as I'm concerned. And I worry that countries approach these things in different ways. I'm sure to not let it happen right now is definitely the right thing. How we achieve that I'm not sure.

RL Are there any circumstances in which you think human cloning might be justified?

IW No.

RL Recently the Human Fertilisation and Embryology Authority has been talking about a condition caused by defects in mitochondrial DNA . . .

IW Some unpleasant diseases are associated with damage to the genetic information in the mitochondria. And so the technical question is can we find a way of combining the genetic information in the egg or the embryo with different mitochondria? If you can do that, I would think that's a great idea, but that doesn't involve making a genetically identical copy of another person. So if you define it as 'would I like genetically identical copies of people?' No. But am I comfortable with the thought of manipulating embryos to improve the health of children? Yes.

RL In the United States there are groups who emphasise individual freedoms, thus individuals should be allowed to reproduce in whatever way they want, given certain conditions, such as love for the child and a commitment to rear the child properly. How would you respond to that argument?

IW You know over the past few years it's obviously become clear to me that you could characterise two broadly different views about society. There is a European view, which is that we should accept that society will tend to regulate a lot of things, including, for example, methods of reproduction. And in the United States there is the view just described that it should be left to the individuals concerned. I do understand both points of view, but over all – I suppose it's predictable – I'm a European in that particular attitude and think that it does make more sense to allow the considered judgements by other people about the way in which these techniques should be used. In this respect, Britain's been very well served by the HFEA and the legislation that brought it into being.

RL Do you support therapeutic cloning?

IW I support very ambitious research into all possible ways of getting treatments for these diseases, so that I'd support research with cells taken from adults, I support research with cells taken from embryos. Many of the latter will be embryos which would otherwise have been destroyed anyway. But in some cases it would be appropriate and necessary to produce the embryos perhaps by cloning in order, for example, to have a particular genotype.

RL Do you think it's unfortunate that we're stuck with the term 'therapeutic'?

IW Yes. You could say that therapeutic cloning for production of embryos by nuclear transfer is a fair term, but it also tends to spread out to include the production of cells from embryos which have been donated, and that's confusing.

RL Getting back to something you said before, in response to those who said you should have fully discussed the implications of your work on Dolly, when you knew it was a possibility, you said that the solution is not to regulate the technology but its applications. Another example I could think of is Los Alamos scientists who worked on the atomic bomb but could not control the consequences of what they'd developed. Do you think there is or there might be a similarity there?

IW No, cloning in its worse possible scenarios is much less threatening than the atomic bomb.

RL . . . but the loss of control which scientists might actually exert over their work . . .

IW I don't know what I would have done, had I been a physicist sixty to seventy years ago. Clearly you can vote with your feet, leave projects if you're not comfortable with what they do and talk about it. I'm not sure, ultimately, if it is for the people doing the research to expect to control the way in which it's used. I think we have an obligation to explain what it is and what we think it will do and its limitations and so on. But why should we be expected to be any smarter than anybody else about making those social and ethical choices? We should note that the same physics which blew up two Japanese cities also produced the electronic equipment you're using to record this interview, and pacemakers, and a thousand other things which we take for granted. There's a much earlier example. The first time somebody put a sharp stone into a stick they could use it to chop firewood, to kill animals to eat or to kill one another. While it's not true to say that every technology has both good and bad, certainly many do. We collectively have to face that fact and to try to see that we get the best out of new opportunities whilst limiting things which are not desirable. I don't think it would work to try to control it in other ways but it would also miss out on opportunities, and if anything frightens me about the public debate about cloning at the present time, it's that the *fear* of the way things might be misused will turn us away from the new opportunities in medicine for treatment of degenerative diseases. And if you list some of the degenerative diseases – stroke, spinal cord injuries, Parkinson's Disease, diabetes, liver damage through hepatitis, a whole range of them – there isn't a fully effective treatment for any of those diseases and in some cases there's no treatment at all. But they're horrible, debilitating conditions. My biggest fear would be that we're frightened away from this. We seem to have a knack as societies of taking for granted what's a few years old but being frightened of what's coming over the future. And there is so much more still to come; we should be excited by it, looking to see what we can do for one another.

RL   How can we decide whether advances such as Dolly should become routinised technology?

IW   There certainly are methods of regulating this. For the foreseeable future in this country cloning in animals would be regulated by the Scientific Procedures Act, which regulates anything experimental done with animals. If you're doing it to produce proteins in milk or organs for people, that will be regulated by the same authority. But at some point, if a technique becomes really routine, it can be moved from that regulation to others; I guess it would be the Veterinary Act which would begin to regulate it. The details of the regulations certainly would vary from one country to another. Take an older technique like artificial insemination which less than sixty years ago caused a very considerable uproar; it would shock people nowadays if they knew just how much difficulty it had caused to the Bishops of the Church of England. That is regulated. You are only allowed to inseminate cattle if you have appropriate training.

RL   Did you expect Dolly to cause such a diversity of reactions?

IW   What we didn't anticipate was the intensity or the duration of interest. If you remember, the story was broken prematurely by the journalists which slightly wrong-footed us. We were planning a press conference during the following week and the story broke on the Sunday. What took us by surprise was just the sheer scale of interest. That was just over five years ago; it was late February. I went away with my wife at Easter that year when the great activity had declined somewhat and remember saying to her that six months from now it would all have gone away. Even at that point I hadn't anticipated quite the extent to which it was going to change the rest of my life. But I'm sure we had thought of the implications; I don't think that there is any potential use of the technology which we have not considered at least a little. We chose not to discuss them all at the beginning, just for the sake of simplification. But we had certainly discussed the implications privately and we then went on to develop them during the following months.

RL How well do you feel cloning has been reported in the media?

IW I think we all know that we live in a world in which the media are subjected to the same market economy as everything else. Inevitably this seems to lead to sensational reporting on almost all occasions. There have been many occasions when, in order to catch a headline, whether it's written or spoken, people have and continue to sensationalise things. I think this is very destructive, not just in relation to cloning. It simplifies and distorts. It would be much better if there wasn't this pressure. There are journalists who will try really hard, and those occasional journalists who will ask you to read pieces for them before they publish them, so it's not quite fair to say that they're all the same. I think it's just typical of the whole of the rest of the media at the present time, that they are distorted by a need for publicity.

RL Where is your work going now?

IW We've spent some time since the announcement trying to develop methods for using the technique in farm animals, with some success. We have cloned pigs; we have made precise genetic changes in sheep. Unfortunately, the lamb that was born was one of the surviving but abnormal animals and in the end it was kinder to euthanise it. It's clear though that what's really needed is an improvement in the effectiveness of the procedure, which is almost equivalent in its scale to the improvement that gave us Dolly. People perceive the cloning of Dolly as being a single experiment. In reality it wasn't of course; it was lots of little steps which were hidden. It's like the iceberg, you know the seven-eighths or whatever that is under the water and then 'pop' out comes the top. A similar thing might happen with future techniques; it may be that they'll be apparent, small increases which will ultimately get you to a good procedure, or it may be that it will be another single big one. To a very great extent, what happens during a nuclear transfer is determined by the nature of the genetic information in the donor cell, the proteins in the oocyte and the way you bring them together, and the succeeding 24 hours or 48 hours. What we're beginning to try to understand is what happens during that process, why does it go wrong so often. Remember, roughly between 1 and 5% will work. So we're beginning to look at cloned embryos. We're beginning to look at cells. Colleagues in Roslin are developing strategies to try to change the cells before we use them and maybe during the use of them. This will be important not only because of its potential use in cloning, but also for cell therapy. We mentioned before that some adult cells have proved to have a wider developmental potential then we'd previously thought. It may also be that if we can understand what the proteins in the oocyte do, we may be able to use that knowledge to enhance that developmental potential even more. This should make it easier to have treatments where you take a cell from a patient, or cells from a patient, treat them, and have them become the type of cell which is needed to treat that condition. So both of those things depend on understanding a lot more about what regulates the functioning of a nucleus and being able to change it.

RL Thank you very much.

Biography

Ian Wilmut is the leader of the team which produced Dolly, the first animal to develop after nuclear transfer from an adult cell. The objectives of the research group are to understand mechanisms which regulate early embryo development and to use that knowledge to establish methods for the multiplication and genetic modification of animals.

5 Pursuing a rational analysis of cloning

Rebecca Bennett and John Harris

What is cloning?

Cloning occurs in nature when an early embryo divides into two separate embryos. These monozygotic twins will be genetically identical. This process can be artificially replicated with similar results. Artificial 'embryo splitting' has been used on humans since 1993 when Jerry Hall and Robert Stillman produced genetically identical embryos by splitting early two- to eight-cell embryos into single embryo cells and then placing them in nutrient solution, when they begin to divide again (Kolberg, 1993). Hall and Stillman produced, on average, three cloned embryos from each original. This technique can be used to provide a 'twin' embryo for biopsy, permitting an embryo undamaged by invasive procedures to be available for implantation following the result of the biopsy of the twin, or to increase the number of embryos available for implantation in the treatment of infertility.

However, it was the possibility of a different kind of cloning, raised by the birth of 'Dolly' the cloned sheep in 1997, that has caused furore in both the scientific and lay communities. The technique of cloning by nuclear transfer involves removing the nucleus of an egg and substituting the nucleus taken from a cell either of another individual or of the egg donor herself. This can be done using cells from an adult. Clones produced by nuclear somatic transfer will not be identical to the nucleus donor. Part of our genetic material comes from the mitochondria in the cytoplasm of the egg and with nuclear somatic transfer only the nuclear DNA is transferred; as a result, the genetic material of the egg donor will partly shape the clone. Moreover, while naturally occurring genetically identical twins have striking similarities, there is no question that they have their own identities and distinct personalities. We are undoubtedly a product of nurture as well as nature, and given this, it is likely that clones who are separated in time from their adult 'twin' are likely to be at least as distinct as naturally occurring genetic twins.

What are the future possibilities?

There are many possible uses for human cloning. Cloning by nuclear somatic transfer offers hope for infertile couples who wish to have a child who is genetically related to one or possibly both of its parents. If the male partner's nuclear DNA were transferred into an egg from his partner, not only would the child be genetically related to its father, the mother would also have contributed to its make up via the influence of the mitochondria.

In contrast to reproductive cloning, 'therapeutic' cloning aims not to produce a new human individual but to create cloned cells which, it is hoped, can be used to treat a number of diseases and disorders. As human embryonic stem cells can potentially develop into any type of cell in the body, their discovery opens up possibilities for the development of lab-grown tissues and organs which could be used to replace tissues and organs damaged by age, disease or trauma. Combining the use of stem cells with nuclear somatic transfer cloning technology may allow the production of replacement tissues and organs which are genetically compatible with the recipient, thus removing the risk of rejection.

In 2001 the first human clones were created by nuclear somatic transfer. Skin cells were taken from volunteers with diseases such as diabetes or spinal cord injury and placed within enucleated embryonic cells to create embryos which were genetic clones of the donors. While the most developed cloned embryo grew to six cells after being cultured for a week, to harvest stem cells for medical use an embryo would need to reach a minimum of 64 cells. However, the US company Advanced Cell Technology responsible for this breakthrough claim that within a decade cloned embryos could have their stem cells harvested to treat a wide variety of conditions, including 'diabetes, stroke, cancer, AIDS, and neurodegenerative disorders such as Parkinson's and Alzheimer's disease' (Lanza, 2001).

What are the current ethical debates about cloning?

Cloning for both reproductive and therapeutic aims has been met with widespread unease from all quarters, including legislative bodies and the scientific community. There are many distinct reasons put forward for this unease, often based on notions of human rights and human dignity. While space here does not allow a sophisticated analysis of the complex debate surrounding cloning, a number of general arguments against cloning have emerged and will be discussed.

Reproductive cloning

In opposition to reproductive cloning it is claimed that the technique would be too dangerous to use on humans. For instance, Dr Harry Griffin, the assistant director of the Roslin Institute, Scotland, which successfully cloned Dolly the sheep argues that:

> It would be irresponsible to try and clone a human being, given the present state of the technology. . . . The chances of success are so low it would be

irresponsible to encourage people to think there's a real prospect. The risks are too great for the woman, and of course for the child.

(Griffin, 2001)

While the predicted success rate associated with cloning humans may be low and there may be risks of producing malformed embryos, against this it could be argued that similar arguments could have been directed against the development of *in vitro* fertilisation techniques (IVF). IVF was once at a stage where success was low but now is an established and valued treatment for infertility which would never have developed if arguments such as this were successfully used to oppose it.

A second source of unease regarding human reproductive cloning arises from worries about the motivation of those who would wish to clone themselves and others. While it might be accepted that human reproductive cloning may provide a way for infertile couples to produce genetically related children, there seems to be a worry that others may use the technique not in order to found a family but in order to reproduce a 'copy' of themselves. Further, there may be those who wish to produce 'copies' of other living or dead individuals. For instance, it was this motivation for cloning that was the focus of the fictional film *The Boys from Brazil*, in which Hitler's genotype was cloned to produce a Fuehrer for the future.

However, any clone of an existing human being will not be a 'copy' of that individual. As we have already discussed, having the same genotype as another individual does not make you the same person as that individual and it is likely that influences from the egg and from the environment would make any clone significantly different from their genetic 'twin'. While this may be so, it could be argued that those who employ reproductive cloning in an attempt (however futile) to produce a copy of themselves or others will not be suitable parents, because of these suspect motives, and that the welfare of any resulting child will suffer. We will return to the welfare of the child in a moment but for now suffice it to say that the motivation many parents have to produce a child may not withstand close scrutiny. What would be a 'good' reason for wishing to have a child? Perhaps all motivations to bring to birth a child are based, at least to some extent, on the selfish wishes of parents? Even if a child is born out of 'suspect' motivations, it seems unlikely to make that child's life unworthwhile, as we will see in a moment.

A third main line of argument against reproductive cloning involves these kinds of worries about the welfare of the resulting child. It may be argued that any child born as a result of nuclear somatic transfer cloning will suffer either because he/she is 'robbed' of his/her genetic identity or because he/she will not have an 'open future'. We will examine these two arguments in turn. In what sense is a cloned individual robbed of his/her genetic identity? While most human individuals are genetically unique, there seems to be no suggestion that permitting the birth of genetically identical monozygotic twins robs anyone of their 'genetic identity' or even that the fact that twins of this kind share a genetic identity is harmful to these individuals. It could be argued, therefore, that it thus seems unclear why this factor should render cloning unethical.

It has been argued (Holm, 1998) that individuals created as a result of nuclear somatic transfer cloning will live their lives in the shadow of their older genetic 'twin' and therefore will not have the 'open future' that most of us have and, it might be claimed, human beings have a right to. Søren Holm, for instance, argues that:

> Usually when a child is born we ask hypothetical questions like 'How will it develop?' or 'What kind of person will it become?' and we often answer them with reference to various psychological traits we can identify in the biological mother or father or in their families . . . In the case of the clone we are, however, likely to give much more specific answers to such questions. Answers that will then go on to affect the way the child is reared.
>
> (Holm, 1998, pp. 160–161)

Holm's argument is that creating a clone that lives life in the shadow of an older genetic twin is unacceptable as:

> It diminishes the clone's possibility of living a life that is in a full sense of that word his or her life. The clone is forced to be involved in an attempt to perform a complicated partial re-enactment of the life of somebody else (the original).
>
> (Holm, 1998, p. 162)

The argument is that while we usually argue for the importance of the principles of respect for individual autonomy or self-determination, we are violating these principles by denying clones this opportunity to live their lives in the way they want to by putting them in a position where they are living in a shadow. However, even if it were true that clones would 'live in the shadow' of their genetic 'originals', it is not clear that this situation should compel us to prohibit cloning.

Arguments which ask us to consider the welfare of a resulting child are problematic. It has been argued that an individual is only wronged by being brought to birth if he/she has a life 'so bad that it would be a cruelty rather than a kindness to bring it into existence' (Bennett and Harris, 2002, p. 323). This kind of blighted existence is sometimes called an 'unworthwhile life'. An 'unworthwhile' life would be a life of overwhelmingly negative experience and thus would only apply in extreme cases of impairment. Other lives which may be less than ideal in all sorts of ways, but not so bad as to deprive that individual of a positive experience of living, are termed 'worthwhile lives'. Thus, the claim is that as long as an individual is likely to have a 'worthwhile life' he/she is not wronged by being brought to birth. However, if an individual is expected to have a life of overwhelming suffering, an unworthwhile life, it is morally wrong to choose to bring such a child to birth. While it may be suggested that this argument is logically difficult as it attempts to compare existence with non-existence, it does seem reasonable to argue that as long as an individual does not have a life so blighted by suffering that it outweighs any pleasure gained by living, that individual has not been wronged by being brought to birth. Thus, even if a clone is likely to have a life that is somehow less than optimal due to its lack of genetic uniqueness or living in the shadow of its 'original', its suffering is unlikely to be such that it renders its life 'unworthwhile'. It could therefore be argued that while being born a clone may not be the optimal way of coming into the world, it is that clone's only chance of existing and existing to have a life which is likely to be worth living. If this argument was accepted, it would establish cloning as ethically acceptable at least on the grounds of the welfare of the child.

Therapeutic cloning

The main objection to therapeutic cloning is the suggestion that it is immoral to create life to be used as a means to an end and then discarded. With therapeutic cloning embryos will be created in order that their stem cells can be harvested and used in an attempt to heal patients with disease, disability and trauma. After these embryos have served their purpose they will be discarded. This kind of claim is often reinforced by appeal to the principle expressed by Immanuel Kant which demands that a human individual should never be thought of solely as a means, but always also as an end. It has been argued, therefore, that '[c]reating human life for the sole purpose of preparing therapeutic material would clearly not be for the dignity of the life created' (Kahn, 1997, p. 119).

In opposition to this view it has been argued (Harris, 1998) that the Kantian principle, invoked without any qualification or gloss, is seldom helpful in medical or bioscientific contexts. The argument is that this principle, especially in its simplistic form, would surely outlaw other established medical procedures normally considered ethically unproblematic. Blood transfusions, for instance, involve using the donor as a means to the end of the recipient. Similarly, an abortion performed exclusively to save the life of the mother would also, presumably, be outlawed by this principle. It can therefore be argued that while Kant's principle does have powerful intuitive force, it is so vague and open to selective interpretation, and its scope for application is consequently so limited, that its utility as one of the fundamental principles of modern ethical thought is virtually zero (Harris, 1998, p. 164).

For example, we often use others as a means to an end. It may be that doing so is only wrong when that person's autonomy is infringed by this action. If a blood donor consents or even volunteers to give blood, then it is not clear that using him as a means to an end is morally suspect. Similarly, it could be argued that using an embryo is equally morally unproblematic, as to do so does not undermine any person's autonomy. On this view the embryo is not a being capable of autonomous choice, and thus using that being as a means to another's end does not wrong the embryo. Further, as using the embryo in this way is likely to benefit others, it is argued that its use in this way should be welcomed. Embryos are constantly created and die in normal sexual reproduction; it is estimated that five embryos are created for every live birth that occurs. It is difficult therefore to object in principle to the creation of embryos for a significant moral purpose.

What is the role of public consultation in the regulation of cloning?

In a report to the British government in 1998 the Human Genetic Advisory Commission and the Human Fertilisation and Embryology Authority claimed 'that for any type of fertility treatment to function satisfactorily there has to be a degree of social acceptance of the measures being taken' (HGAC/HFEA, 1998, section 4, para 4.8). The report then continues that it is quite clear that human reproductive cloning is unacceptable to a substantial majority of the population and concludes that:

> A total ban on its use for any purposes is the obvious and straightforward way of recognising this. The results of the consultation fully support the government policy in this respect.
>
> (HGAC/HFEA, 1998)

For this report the two committees attempted a public consultation exercise, that is they tried to find out what the public thought about human reproductive cloning and they fed the results of this consultation, which were only negative, back to the report. Public bodies deliberating on ethical questions often involve 'consultation exercises'. Of course, no one can object to public consultation; the public should be consulted, democracy requires it. However, while public consultations may be useful in providing information on the public's reaction to a development, it is controversial as to whether these consultations are of value to the ethical debate.

What weight should be given to the results of public consultations on cloning? If the majority of the community appear to find human reproductive cloning unacceptable, is this a sufficient reason to impose a total ban on this technique? There are those who argue that ultimately morality is a personal and subjective matter, and as such one person's beliefs are as good as another's and it is impossible to choose between them. As Tim Dare puts it

> Very crudely, the idea is that in ethics there are merely opinions, and that as a result no one can give authoritative advice as to what is right and what is wrong. . . . Each person's assessment of the right thing to do is in this sense at least as good as anyone else's. . . .
>
> (Dare, 1998, p. 184)

On this view public consultation would provide an acceptable way of determining what is the morally right course with regard to cloning. The public are consulted and their opinions are gauged, providing a picture, on this view, of what is morally acceptable and what isn't. However, there is a strong argument that suggests that public consultations, while interesting, do not contribute to the quest for truth regarding the morality of cloning or any other issue. On this view it is argued that discovering what the public thinks about issues of ethical significance is not the same as discovering the ethical values of the public, and finding out what the public thinks it acceptable to do about issues of ethical significance does not necessarily produce ethical judgements.

The argument here is that it is not usually possible to determine whether the result of public consultation gives an account of the ethical judgements of the public or of their unsubstantiated opinions. There is no room to analyse in any detail here what makes something an ethical judgement as opposed to an unsubstantiated opinion, but we can say that it is the role of reason and the willingness to justify a judgement with evidence and argument which distinguishes an ethical judgement. Thus, on this view, while the nature of medical dilemmas is often such that they produce strong feelings from those who encounter them, these feelings are not sufficient to solve these dilemmas. James Rachels points out that these feelings may be nothing but the products of prejudice, selfishness or cultural conditioning and argues that:

> if we want to discover the truth, we must try to let our feelings be guided as much as possible by the reasons, or arguments, that can be given for the opposing views. Morality is, first and foremost, a matter of consulting reason: the morally right thing to do, in any circumstance, is determined by what there are the best reasons for doing.
>
> (Rachels, 1993, p. 10)

By applying the techniques and principles of moral philosophy to these practical dilemmas, applied ethics aims not only to enable better understanding of the nature of moral problems but also to try to resolve them. Instead of basing our decisions about these dilemmas on our unsubstantiated feelings, the clarification and investigation of concepts and beliefs enable the arguments on all sides to be evaluated in an attempt to produce the best answer to the problem, an answer based on reasons rather than feelings. Thus, on this view it is the role of reason that distinguishes moral judgements from personal tastes.

Furthermore, there is often a tendency towards conservatism in the results of public consultations. On one view it may be argued that by giving force to often conservative public consultations we are proceeding responsibly, exposing communities to the least danger. However, against this it might be argued that in many cases the failure to accept new technologies, such as the production of stem cells by cloning, may be the policy of most harm in the long term, missing valuable opportunities for benefit. If this precautionary approach may be based on little more than unsubstantiated opinion, then there may be an argument to decrease the influence of public consultation on policy in such cases.

References

Bennett, R. and Harris, J. (2002) Are there lives not worth living? When is it morally wrong to reproduce?, in Donna L. Dickenson (Ed.) *Ethical Issues in Maternal-Fetal Medicine* (Cambridge, Cambridge University Press), pp. 321–34.
Dare, T. (1998) Applied ethics, challenges to, in Ruth Chadwick (Ed.) *Encyclopedia of Applied Ethics, Volume 1* (New York: Academic Press).
Griffin, H. (2001) Interview for *BBC Online* published on Tuesday 30 January 2001, 17.08 GMT at http://news.bbc.co.uk/hi/english/sci.
Harris, J. (1998) Cloning and human dignity, *Cambridge Quarterly of Healthcare Ethics* 7, 163–7.
HGAC/HFEA (1998) *Cloning: Issues in Reproductive Science and Medicine* (www. doh.gov.uk/hgac/papers/papers-d.htm section9).
Holm, S. (1998) A life in the shadow: one of the reasons why we should not clone humans, *Cambridge Quarterly of Healthcare Ethics* 7, 160–62.
Kahn, A. (1997) Clone mammals . . . clone man, *Nature* 386, 119.
Kolberg, R. (1993) Human embryo cloning reported, *Science*, New Series, Vol. 262, No. 5134 (Oct. 29), pp. 652–3.
Lanza, R. (2001) [Vice President of US company Advanced Cell Technology] quoted in *Guardian*, 26 November (www.guardian.co.uk/international/story/0,3604,606009. html).
Rachels, J. (1993) *The Elements of Moral Philosophy*, 2nd Edition (New York: McGraw Hill).

Further reading

Justine Burley and John Harris (Eds) *A Companion to Genethics: Philosophy and the Genetic Revolution* (Oxford: Basil Blackwell, 2001).
John Harris *Clones, Genes and Immortality* (Oxford: Oxford University Press, 1998).
Justine Burley (Ed.) *The Genetic Revolution and Human Rights: In Support of Amnesty International* (Oxford: Oxford University Press, 1999).

Biography

Rebecca Bennett is Lecturer in Bioethics and Fellow of the Institute of Medicine, Law and Bioethics. She is currently developing materials for the MA/Postgraduate Diploma in Health Care Ethics and Law by Distributed Learning. She has published widely on diverse issues in bioethics.

John Harris is Sir David Alliance Professor of Bioethics at the Institute of Medicine, Law and Bioethics, University of Manchester. He is a member of the United Kingdom Human Genetics Commission and of the Ethics Committee of the British Medical Association. He was one of the founder directors of the International Association of Bioethics and a founder member of the board of the journal *Bioethics* and a member of the editorial board of the *Journal of Medical Ethics* and many other journals.

6 Cloning? Yuk!

David King

Introduction

A book entitled *Key Issues in Bioethics* clearly should address the subject of cloning because cloning provides an exceptionally stark example of the failure of conventional academic bioethics to provide an understanding of the crucial issues, and of what is at stake. In the face of overwhelming public opposition to cloning, and a set of simple and obvious reasons for not permitting it, the real question is not 'what's wrong with cloning?' but 'what's wrong with bioethics?'.

We are faced here with a discourse problem. For reasons that I will expand on, academic bioethics must eliminate from its discourse any arguments that are concerned with the historical, social and economic trends that lead to the appearance of scientific discoveries and technologies, and which determine their moral and social meaning and impact. Yet it is precisely these social appreciations of the issue which are expressed in the entirely valid popular yuk! reaction to cloning.

I will argue that cloning represents a particularly clear example of a long term trend: the denaturing and commodification of human reproduction through its increasing dependence on technology. This trend not only dehumanises people and ultimately undermines human rights, but is driven by and reinforces ongoing eugenic processes which, if allowed to proceed unchecked, will prove disastrous for society.

There is little that is new in the argument that cloning dehumanises. This point has been made most convincingly by Leon Kass (Kass, 1997), and much of this article echoes his concerns. What Kass' analysis lacks, because he is a conservative, is a critical understanding of technology politics, and I will try to remedy this defect here.

The case against cloning

The reason for banning human cloning is that it is an especially blatant example of the trend in Western capitalist societies towards the denaturing and commodification of human reproduction that I have already mentioned. Allowed to proceed unchecked, this trend will produce a society which most humans alive today would find unliveable. We are on a slippery slope. The slope began about 400 years ago, began sloping downwards more steeply about 100 years ago, took a major dive around 40 years ago, and with cloning threatens to become precipitous. The nature of slippery slopes is that people only notice they are on them and react when there is a change in the gradient. This is why there is such a fuss about cloning.

The trend I am referring to can be described most simply as the reconfiguring of human reproduction as a capitalist industrial production process. It is just one example of a broader process which is constitutive of capitalist societies, and is conventionally described as progress: the dismantling of all barriers to the exploitation and control of nature and the reconfiguration of natural processes according to the model of commodity production and trade. That is why I dated the origins of the cloning crises to the Scientific Revolution of the seventeenth century and the beginning of modern capitalism.

What makes cloning an especially clear example of the industrialisation of reproduction is, of course, the fact that it can mass-produce genetic uniformity, according to the Fordist model. Whereas sexual reproduction results in new-ness, variation, unpredictability and uniqueness, cloning produces sameness, predictability and control. It is this feature which decisively distinguishes clon-ing from *in vitro* fertilisation (IVF) and other technologies that assist sexual reproduction. The unnaturalness of cloning, its impossibility in the normal course of biological events, and the novel biological, social and ethical conse-quences of breaking biological rules, mean that it is qualitatively different from IVF, and so should be our reaction to it.

One biological consequence of this rule-breaking is the high death rate and the 'big offspring phenomenon' observed in cloned animals (McEvoy *et al.*, 2002; Chavatte-Palmer *et al.*, 2000). This appears to spring directly from the rule that mammals shall have one male parent and one female, and that repro-duction shall occur through the union of haploid cells produced by meiosis. (These problems are the main, official, ethical barrier to cloning.) The rules of mammalian reproduction arise from the integrated character of biological processes, which have been tuned by billions of years of evolution. Faced with such a clear result of breaking natural laws, it is not surprising that people complain that cloning is unnatural and question scientists' drive to dismantle all natural constraints, whatever the cost.

Kass and others have argued convincingly that the new genetic uniqueness that results from the randomness of sexual reproduction is a crucially important and constitutive aspect of being human. (It should be noted that monozygotic twins do not refute this principle; they merely provide a minor exception to it – identical twins' genotypes arise randomly, not calculatedly, and are new com-pared to any previous human genotypes, including their parents.) The fact that we are new, unknown and different from anyone who has gone before commands respect and equal treatment: it compels others to take us for what we are, and not to imagine they have the measure of us. This is an important part of the basis of human rights.

A more important aspect of producing humans, rather than conceiving them, is objectification. Whereas sexual reproduction gives rise to human subjects, cloning produces objects: rather than arising from a random, natural process over which we have no control, clones are the products of human design (more strictly, selection). This can only put them in a subordinate position relative to their selector/designer, a position that corresponds to that of an object *vis-à-vis* a subject. The selector, who chooses which genome to replicate, assumes total control of another human being's genetic essence. With cloning, although we do not yet design the genome, as would the genetic engineer, we have a degree of control much greater than is available to a genetic engineer working with sexually conceived embryos. Unlike prenatal genetic testing, a form of 'negative control' where we simply choose to consign certain future people to non-existence, cloning is a form of positive control over the entire content of an individual's genome.

I would argue that this objectification undermines the clone's ethical status *vis-à-vis* all other humans, not just their parent/designer. Of course, cloned humans should, in theory, be treated as persons, like any other. But clones will be compromised in that crucial feature of human subjecthood that determines our ethical relationship with them. A human subject is simply unconditionally herself, equal and other to us and belonging only to herself: she must be treated as an equal, with her own interests. As objects, clones will not belong to themselves. Perhaps the ethical status of clones would be somewhat more like that of farm animals, whose reproduction is rigorously controlled by their superiors. By imagining how we would react to, say, fifty clones of the same person, it is easy to see how the industrial character of their origins would erode the ethical seriousness with which we would relate to them. I would contend that this is no less the case with a single clone. One might say, following Marx, that if the control by others of one's labour power produces alienation, then how much more so would the control of one's genome and the incorporation of one's genetic being into the production process.

The replacing of natural means of reproduction with technology is also a eugenic trend, for as it becomes more technological, reproduction and its products must conform more and more to industrial/technological criteria of predictability/uniformity, quality control and efficiency. Although it has often been misunderstood as a right-wing phenomenon, eugenics, in its heyday, was supported by many liberals and leftists, who viewed it as modern, humane and progressive. What united their vision with right-wing authoritarians was a vision of social control through regulation of the unpredictable mess caused by reproduction. In its essence, eugenics is the capitalist project of control of nature applied to human reproduction (King, 1997), and has always depended for its realisation upon medical and technological intervention in reproduction. This began with sterilisation, family planning/contraception and abortion and intensified through IVF, prenatal screening, preimplantation genetic diagnosis and now cloning. The often-predicted goal of this progression is the complete separation of sex from reproduction, and an artificial reproduction with gestation *in vitro* and genetic engineering.

The technologisation of reproduction is also necessary for another form of distortion: commercialisation. This is already evident in the buying and selling of babies in commercial surrogacy, and the selling of eggs from 'genetically superior' women on the Internet. Several putative cloning companies aim to charge up to $200,000 per cloned baby. But in cloning the degree of technical intervention involved makes not only the process but also the product, a human embryo, patentable. Several companies have now claimed cloned human embryos as their intellectual property. Human embryos become, literally, commodities to be bought and sold. One does not have to believe that embryos are persons (I do not) to feel that this degrades the dignity of human life.

In summary, I have argued that cloning is the latest step in the techno-eugenicist, capitalist trend in human reproduction. Trying to control reproduction to such a degree, according to criteria that are alien to it, can only do violence to its biological and social function – the creation of unique human subjects. Cloning turns us from unique subjects to be accepted unconditionally into designed, produced and selected objects, to be bought, sold and judged according to eugenic criteria. Dehumanisation does not seem too strong a word.

Is it any wonder that people cry out, inarticulately, 'Yuk!' at this distortion of their basic structures of meaning and human values? Is it any wonder that they decry the unnaturalness of cloning and deplore those who want to control life in this way, and set themselves up over it, as 'playing God'? Our bioethicists are by now well-practised in the art of debunking these unphilosophical expressions of outrage, pointing out the many ways in which we already play God, and how our concepts of what is natural are socially constructed. But what ordinary people see, and our clever experts miss, because they are themselves so deeply a part of the technocratic enterprise, is the degrading overall trend. And the whole point of that trend *is* limitless control, and its method *is* the dismantling and exploitation of the natural. That trend must be stopped at the point of cloning, for if we fail to control it, its control of us will become unbreakable. We are at one of those points on the slippery slope where, bioethicists always insist, it will be possible to dig our heels in and say, 'Thus far and no further'. We must do so, and the bioethicists should muck in and help.

Some more detailed arguments

The psychology of clones

In the cloning debate there has been much talk of the psychological problems of clones. Kass, in time-honoured conservative fashion, makes much of the problems caused by subversion of the normal patterns of kinship. Others have talked about the problems of lack of genetic uniqueness, and being expected to conform to your genetic heritage. It certainly does not seem implausible that, as with some monozygotic twins, the genetic sameness will be reinforced with an attempt to impose the same environment and experiences. This is especially obvious with the stereotypical egomaniac self-cloner, but is likely to be an unconscious part of the behaviour of all cloning parents, unless they make a positive effort to do otherwise. A genetic copy of a father is likely to have his genetic predispositions reinforced in the nicest possible way. All parents do this to some degree, but the tendency seems likely to be considerably more pronounced with clones. The very fact of objectifying a person in this way, and of placing oneself in the position of designer, will tend to encourage this. As Kass says, where ordinary parents have hopes, cloners will have expectations. And knowing that the content of your genome is known and predetermined in advance, that you are in the subordinate position of designed object, is hardly likely to enhance a child's resistance to parental domination – unless it produces extreme rejection of the parent.

While very real, these concerns are hard to evaluate. Cloning would interfere with fundamental aspects of the human condition: kinship, genetic uniqueness and subjecthood. Twins often have psychological challenges, but they do not have to cope with the added difficulties of radically disturbed kinship, and being a designed object. However, human psychology is complex and experience has surely taught that people can make the best of many kinds of bad job. We cannot predict exactly how the parents of clones will behave. In my view concerns about psychology are not a decisive objection to human cloning. However, we can surely say that this is a very bad job to have to make the best of. Cloning is likely to produce alienation in the psychological sense of the word. British law requires the regulator to consider the welfare of the child in deciding whether to permit the use of IVF – it seems unlikely that cloning would pass this test.

Clones aren't real copies (so there's nothing to worry about)

In the wake of the Dolly furore, many experts were keen to assure us that a clone of Mel Gibson would not be another Mel Gibson. The clone's pre- and post-natal environment and experiences would produce a different person (Lewontin, 1998). This is, of course, true as far as it goes and indeed cloning cannot produce the same uniformity as an industrial production line. But, as identical twins show us, genes really do matter, which is why would-be cloners are so keen to replicate them. Few scientists would now support the 'blank slate' model of human beings of the 1950s.

However, the real fallacy in this argument is the same as that involved in the objection that twins are clones and that there is no problem with twins (Bailey, 1998). The objection is not to sameness *per se*, but to its attempted imposition by outsiders, especially when this is part of a larger trend of rewriting reproduction according to an industrial script. Actions are made illegitimate not only by their consequences but also by the motivation of the actors and the contexts which frame them.

Reproductive liberty

It is often argued, especially in the USA, that people have a 'right to reproduce in any way they want', which is reinforced by a strong belief that the state has no role to play in personal matters such as reproduction. There may be a 'negative right' of non-interference in one's right to 'marry and found a family' as the Universal Declaration of Human Rights puts it. However, that is a very different thing from asserting a positive right of access to any technological means necessary to have a child, simply because one happens to *want* to use a particular reproductive method, no matter what the consequences for the child or for society. (I would suggest that the inability to recognise this obvious distinction is due to the pervasive influence of an individualistic consumerist ethic, which insists that we have the right to anything we want and no-one shall be allowed to interfere with our pursuit of our desires.) The point is that there is no right to have a child if doing so, in any particular way, violates important social goals. We cannot pretend that reproduction exists in some inviolable bubble immune from normal considerations – it has always been a highly social activity, subject to innumerable social and cultural constraints.

Cloning is inevitable and cannot be banned

In the public discussion on cloning it is often suggested that there is some inevitability about cloning, and that attempts to ban it are futile. This is usually based on the idea that 'you can't stop science', or that nations cannot prevent the actions of maverick 'mad scientists'.

Strictly speaking, of course, this is not an argument about whether it is right to try to ban cloning. However, it does deserve attention because it is factually incorrect, and has a major impact on the debate. Science is anything but a juggernaut, proceeding inexorably according to its own internal logic, in a social vacuum. The agenda of scientific research is driven by many social factors, especially economic competition between nations and companies. Science with little commercial applicability rarely happens, because it does not get funded. It is ironic that those who believe that 'you can't stop science' present themselves as wise to the ways of the world, yet understand so little of how science really works. It is they, not those who believe cloning can be banned, who are the naïve idealists.

As for the maverick scientist, cloning events may or may not take place before there is a global ban, with severe penalties attached. In my judgement they will not, because the technical difficulties will delay success until after a ban is passed. But even if I am wrong, there is a major difference between a world in which an isolated cloning event occurs, and the cloner goes to jail, and one in which cloning becomes an accepted economic activity. Since I prefer the former scenario I will continue to lobby for a ban. At present the United Nations has taken up the call, and there is every reason to believe that cloning will be banned worldwide by 2005. At the national level, in response to a perceived threat, legislation can be passed in days.

It is interesting to ask why people seem so keen to proclaim themselves powerless. The often-voiced sentiment that 'you can't stop progress' reveals our postmodern ambivalence towards the capitalist technocracy that dominates our lives. On the one hand, we have stopped believing in anything, especially our own ability to change the world for the better, and we are rightly sceptical about dominant narratives of progress. The fashionable pose is a worldly wise cynicism. On the other hand, we cannot altogether give up our belief in progress, and can only hope desperately that more technology will bring something better. So we accept technologisation uneasily, feeling alternately hopeful and victimised, but always powerless in the face of technocracy.

Cloning should be allowed for infertility treatment

In most people's eyes the most serious reason for permitting cloning is for infertility treatment for those who lack sperm or eggs. It is a measure of how far we have fallen under the spell of the moral blackmail of the infertility industry that we are prepared to entertain this. First, why do we no longer question the assumption that people must have children that are 100% genetically related to (in this case only one of) them? Why can such couples not accept sperm or egg donation or adoption as alternatives?

More importantly, we must resist the moral blackmail. We must insist that the relief of infertility does not justify crossing a fundamental barrier, which will have drastic consequences for humanity. Any bioethics worthy of the name must be able to insist that medical advancement does not justify *any* means.

How many clones are too many?

An approach that has had little airing but in my view is very powerful is to ask the following questions of those who would accept cloning: how many clones of one person should be permitted, and on what basis? Even the most ardent libertarian advocates of cloning tend to balk at the idea of making fifty or even ten copies of one person, yet on their own arguments there is little justification for such scruples. As soon as one starts to argue that ten clones are not acceptable, one is forced to accept that there is something inappropriate about creating humans by simple replication and that this might have harmful consequences for society. But where does one draw the line, and on what basis? Why would it be acceptable to create two copies, but not three or six? The only remotely plausible place to draw the line is at one copy of the individual, so that the clone is not too different from ordinary humans. Yet even this would be vulnerable to the argument that twins and some triplets are clones, so what's the problem in making two or three clones? Aside from the philosophical difficulties, the supporters of cloning will have to show how, in practical terms, they would prevent multiple cloning once cloning was permitted. In fact, multiple cloning would be likely to happen immediately, because if IVF practice were followed, as would likely be necessary given the highly inefficient and experimental nature of cloning, at least two or three cloned embryos would need to be implanted.

What's wrong with bioethics?

Although a few bioethicists have taken strong positions opposed to cloning, the majority of Anglo-American bioethicists, including the US National Bioethics Advisory Commission (NBAC, 1997), have been unable to see strong reasons for not permitting cloning, beyond safety concerns which are expected to be temporary. I would suggest this failure reveals something significant about bioethics itself.

The main failing of contemporary Anglo-American bioethics is its apparent treatment of issues in a social vacuum. I have been unable to find any discussion of cloning that sets it in the proper social and historical context. Conventional academic bioethics also appears to have a rule that arguments about societal concerns can barely be mentioned, and can certainly never override its key concern for individual autonomy. The excessive stress on autonomy (especially in the USA) and the exclusion of consideration of social impact give us a clue that academic bioethics is far from attaining the 'apolitical neutrality' it claims. In fact, what we are dealing with in bioethical debates are discussions between different strands of liberalism. Amongst political ideologies, liberalism has always succeeded best in portraying itself as 'simple common sense', and as not reflecting any particular set of social interest groups.

What is interesting is the way that bioethics' stance of political neutrality, and its exclusion of social analysis, exactly parallel the liberal ideology of science itself, whereby science is supposedly objective, neutral and divorced from social and political influences. This self-image is vital in allowing scientists not to notice the ways in which science serves the interests of capitalism in a hundred subtle and less subtle ways. It would appear that the same trick of self-deception works even in discussions, which, unlike science, are supposed to be about values.

I would argue that the reason that official bioethics fails to interrogate the long-term techno-historical trend (or slippery slope) is precisely because of its role within that trend. It has succeeded in constructing a liberal discourse that excludes issues of social power and how it is exercised, for example through control of technological agendas. But by failing to fundamentally critique biomedical definitions of progress, it has become slave to the biomedical paradigm. The traditional critique of liberalism is as true of bioethics: those who fail to critique power end up serving it.

This does not mean that bioethicists slavishly follow a party line dictated to them by scientists, or that all bioethicists are simple spin doctors for biomedical technology and the vested interests behind it. Bioethics has space for the most earnest and well-meaning liberals, who take ethics just as seriously as they should be. In fact, debate is encouraged, and the fact that it takes place, albeit on an 'expert level' supposedly beyond the understanding of the public, is always given as the main reason that the public should be reassured: 'Don't worry, we've set up an ethics committee and our experts are looking into it.' Of course, as is often remarked, such committees substitute for real public debate. But the key point is that these expert discussions are always subject to the structural constraints of the bioethics discourse. The exclusion of issues of power and social control means that, at least in Britain and the US, bioethics has achieved the status of neutral arbiter and protector of values. Bioethicists, but never critical sociologists, are allowed to advise government.

However, the problem with the discourse and role chosen for bioethics, as many commentators have noted, is that they produce an inability to ever say no, on the basis of firm values. With cloning, as with successive developments on the biomedical slippery slope, it is always impossible to find consensus against the latest step in eugenic commodification. As Kass notes, although we are always reassured that each step is acceptable, because we will be able to say no to something worse further along, when that thing arrives we are shamelessly told that we have already accepted, for example IVF, so how can we object to cloning? Within the unquestioned ideology of progress, resistance is ascribed to inconsistent irrationality and a fear of the new, which will doubt-less fade away in time.

In *The Communist Manifesto* Marx remarks that the experience of life in a capitalist society is that 'everything solid melts into air'. This does not 'just happen' by itself – there is a well paid and intelligent group of people whose job it is to make sure that it happens. It is ironic in the extreme that this same group of poachers has taken upon itself the role of gamekeeper and has succeeded in convincing us that the problem is 'Science running out of control, while ethics strives to put on the brake'. Nowadays, the solution to every problem is to set up an ethics committee, but somehow no-one ever notices how little braking power these committees seem to possess. We can, with justification, ask them the following question: if they cannot bring themselves to say no to cloning, what will they ever say no to?

Note

Please note that the views expressed in this article are Dr King's personal opinions and do not represent the policy of Human Genetics Alert.

References

Bailey, R. (1998) The twin paradox: what exactly is wrong with cloning?, in McGee, G. (Ed.) *The Human Cloning Debate* (Berkeley, Berkeley Hill Books).

Chavatte-Palmer, P., Heyman, Y. and Renard, J. P. (2000) Cloning and associated physiopathology of gestation, *Gynecology Obstetrics and Fertility* 28, pp. 633–42.

Kass, L. (1997) The wisdom of repugnance, *The New Republic*, 2 June, pp. 17–26.

King, D. (1997) Eugenic tendencies in modern genetics, in Sutton, A. (Ed.) *Man Made Man* (Dublin, Four Courts Press).

Lewontin, R. (1998) The confusion over cloning, in McGee, G. (Ed.) *The Human Cloning Debate* (Berkeley, Berkeley Hill Books).

McEvoy, T. G., Sinclair, K. D., Young, L. E., Wilmut, I. and Robinson, J. J. (2002) Large offspring syndrome and other consequences of ruminant embryo culture in vitro: relevance to blastocyst culture in human ART, *Human Fertility* 3, pp. 238–46.

NBAC (1997) *Cloning Human Beings* (Rockville, Maryland).

Further reading

Andrews, L. B. (1999) *The Clone Age: adventures in the new world of reproductive technology* (New York, Henry Holt).

Appleyard, B. (1998) *Brave New Worlds: staying human in the genetic future* (New York, Viking).

Buchanan, A., Brock, D. W., Daniels, N. and Wikler, D. (2000) *From Chance to Choice: genetics and justice* (New York, Cambridge University Press).

Kolata, G. (1998) *Clone: the road to Dolly and the path ahead* (New York, Morrow and Co.).

Maranto, G. (1996) *Quest for Perfection: the drive to breed better human beings* (New York, Scribner).

Nussbaum, M. C. and Sunstein C. R. (Eds) (1998) *Clones and Clones: facts and fantasies about human cloning* (New York, Norton).

Pence, G. (Ed.) (1998) *Flesh of My Flesh: the ethics of cloning humans – a reader* (Rowman and Littlefield, Lanham, MD).

Biography

David King is Coordinator of Human Genetics Alert, a watchdog group focusing on ethical and social issues raised by human genetics. He was formerly editor of *GenEthics News* and Director of the Genetics Forum. He has a PhD in molecular biology from Edinburgh University and a BA from Christ's College, Cambridge. He is a member of the Ethics Group of the North Cumbria Community Genetics Project. He has written for many publications and is a regular contributor to TV and radio current affairs programmes on genetics.

7 Clones and cloning

New reproductive futures

Sarah Franklin

The issue of cloning attracted increasing public attention in the late 1990s, in large part due to the production of Dolly the sheep at the Roslin Institute in Scotland in 1996 by Ian Wilmut and his team of scientists working in close collaboration with Scotland's leading biotechnology company, PPL Therapeutics. The novel technique used to produce Dolly confirmed the viability of a new kind of biological reproduction by successfully merging an *adult* cell from one female sheep (a mammary cell) with an egg cell from another sheep to create a fully viable embryo. Before the cloning of mammals in the 1990s such a means of reproduction was considered out of the question because it was assumed that an egg cell could only be fertilised by a sperm and when cloning was achieved it could only materialise through the fusion of a young fetal cell with an enucleated egg cell. Using sophisticated techniques of molecular engineering and micromanipulation, Wilmut's team produced a live, healthy offspring, Dolly, whose viability confirmed the utility of a process known as somatic cell nuclear transfer (CNR).

Somatic cells are distinguished from germ cells because they are the differentiated cells that make up all of the distinct types of tissue in the body. A key principle of biological development that was challenged by the success of the Dolly experiment is the assumption that it is one-way and irreversible. In other words, it was assumed that once a cell committed itself to a particular developmental pathway, by specialising to become a specialised cell type, it could not, as it were, 'go back in time' to provide the complete set of genetic instructions necessary to produce a new embryo. This function was previously believed to belong exclusively to germ cells, that is, only to eggs and sperm.

A key discovery enabling adult, differentiated cells to serve as partner cells to germ cells involved the role of cell cytoplasm. Cytoplasm is often described as the gelatinous 'soup' in which all of the cell's distinct organelles, such as mitochondria, ribosomes and the nucleus, are immersed. The cytoplasm of egg cells is particularly powerful, in part because the egg cell (ovum) is the largest of all mammalian cells – 100 times larger, for example, than the mammary cell with which it was fused to create Dolly. After slowing down an ovum and a mammary cell to the G0 phase of their cycles, known as quiescence, and equivalent to cellular sleep, Roslin scientists injected the entire mammary cell from a Finn

Dorset ewe into an ovum from a Blackface ewe, from which the nucleus, containing its nuclear DNA or genetic blueprint, had been removed. Using an electrical apparatus to restart the cell cycle, jolting the newly united cells out of their sleep phase, a new, reconstructed cell was capacitated, developing to become an embryo, which was carried by two additional surrogate sheep during gestation. The viability of this new technique of cellular merger was confirmed when Dolly was born as a healthy and normal lamb, although in 277 other cases the same technique failed.

According to Ian Wilmut, the cytoplasm of the egg cell is so powerful it can, in effect, 'reset the clock' of adult DNA, restoring its original capacities to provide the instructions for any kind of cell – and indeed all of the cells necessary to create a viable offspring. The analogy used by Wilmut is that the egg cell cytoplasm 'reprogrammes' adult DNA. It is this capacity to reprogramme one kind of cell to become another that has been seen to offer significant possibilities for growing replacement tissue, such as liver, skin or other organs, which have both medical and commercial potential in the field now known as regenerative medicine.

What has come to be called 'the Dolly technique', also known as nuclear transfer technology, is increasingly widely used to create what are described as 'reconstructed cells'. These cells are in turn used to create cell lines and cell cultures which have a wide range of potential applications. Among these is the potential for an individual's own cells to be used to produce spare parts in the event of major illness or organ failure. Whereas, in the past, significant problems of tissue rejection have hampered the progress of transplantation, the new techniques offer the possibility of a kind of bespoke medicine which uses a person's own tissue to create new means of repairing damaged organs. For example, skin tissue could be used to create replacement heart tissue – and in a manner that bypasses the problem of rejection, because the new cells are a perfect tissue match (histocompatible).

Cellular reconstruction techniques, or what is now known as the field of tissue engineering, is complex and at an early stage, so that it is anticipated many of the benefits of this new field will not be available for at least ten, if not fifty, years. Moreover, the field is very controversial, because experimentation requires the use of both adult and embryonic cells (e.g. Lovell-Badge, 2001). For some religious groups, the use of human embryonic tissue is unacceptable under any conditions – even if, for example, the embryos come from *in vitro* fertilisation programmes, and are available for research because couples have donated the embryos they no longer wish to use or keep in storage (Franklin, 1999). In contrast, many members of the medical and scientific professions have lobbied intensively, and in Britain successfully, to allow limited use of human embryos to explore medical applications of cloning technology in the pursuit of future cures and treatments for disease.

There are thus two main sources of opposition to human cloning. One set of objections surrounds the possibility of using the Dolly technique to clone a baby or adult (Silver, 1999). Although some experts in the field of assisted conception have argued cloning should be available as an additional method to overcome childlessness for those couples who desire to attempt it, other scientists, including Ian Wilmut, strongly oppose such proposals, arguing the technique is at too early a stage in development to be used safely or reliably. Having witnessed the birth of several lambs who have suffered from significant, often fatal, abnormalities as a result of having been created through the Dolly technique, Ian Wilmut argues it is immoral to risk producing a human being by this means (see Chapter 4). Such a person might be born with very serious, untreatable and unprecedented types of congenital malformations.

Many scientists who oppose the use of cloning for human reproduction, however, strongly support the use of cloning for a second, more limited, set of medical purposes – in particular for growing human tissues to be used for a range of therapeutic purposes – in spite of objections to the use of human embryos (reconstructed or otherwise) for experimental purposes. To devise regulatory policy, a distinction has been drawn between reproductive cloning and therapeutic cloning by advisory bodies such as the Human Fertilisation and Embryology Authority, who recommend that reproductive cloning be banned under any circumstances, but that stem cell research using the Dolly technique to create reconstructed embryos be allowed under licence when human embryonic tissue is involved.

Cloning is a somewhat misleading term for all of these developments because its definition is imprecise. Etymologically, cloning derives from the Greek word for twig, referring to the process by which a new plant can often be created from a cutting. Cloning thus, classically, refers to the creation of a new organism from only one parent. Technically, this does not accurately categorise Dolly the sheep, who was created from a merger of two cells from two different animals. Although DNA fingerprinting has definitively established that Dolly's nuclear genetic material is 100% derived from the adult cell which came from one animal, and although she has all of the familiar characteristics of a Finn Dorset, not a Blackface, sheep, it is confusing to refer to Dolly as a 'clone' in the strict sense of the term, because her origins are more complex. What 'cloning' means in the case of Dolly is that she has been born via the process of nuclear transfer, and that her consequent nuclear genetic identity with one parent makes her a 'clone'. However, if one of the main implications of Dolly's birth is that the relationship between nuclear genetic material and its surrounding cellular environment is much more complex, and interactive, than was previously assumed, then she must be seen as unique. In other words, it is somewhat misleading to describe Dolly as identical to her genetic parent, since this would suggest *it is only DNA which creates individuality*. Although the association of a person's DNA with his or her individual uniqueness is often emphasised in accounts of sexual reproduction and biological development, the Dolly technique demonstrates that, as in the case of genetically identical twins, individuality is more than merely genetic.

In the future, cloning will play an increasing role in the production of new living organisms. An expanding toolkit of cellular reconstruction techniques will enable an increasingly broad range of recombinant organisms to be produced with increasing molecular precision, for a wide range of potential applications – from the production of improved milk for infants (nutriceuticals) to new drugs, and new cell lines. Dolly was initially created as part of a process of exploring new forms of animal breeding, and her birth represents an intensification of animal domestication. In creating Dolly, Roslin scientists were initially attempting to devise new means of reproducing dairy animals that have had useful human genes added to their nuclear DNA, so that they can produce the specific enzymes that are missing in people who suffer from disabling genetic conditions, such as cystic fibrosis. For example, using *in vitro* fertilisation techniques, a female sheep embryo can be implanted with a human gene carrying the instructions to make alpha-1-antitrypsin (AAT), and then gestated to become a ewe with the capacity to excrete this valuable enzyme in her milk. Enzymes extracted from the milk of such sheep can thus be used to make new pharmaceutical products aimed at replacing the enzyme that is missing in people who suffer from specific genetic diseases. AAT was the first pharmaceutical of this kind to be licensed in Britain, by PPL Therapeutics in May 2000,[1] for use in the treatment of cystic fibrosis – which is the most common genetic disorder in Western Europe. Animals who produce medicines in this way are known as 'bio-reactors', and it was, in part, the attempt to produce such sheep more efficiently and reliably that led to the discovery of the Dolly technique.

In turn, the Dolly technique has been rapidly expanded, so that, in combination with other new and established methods, it now comprises one of the basic procedures for the biotechnology industry. This industry is itself often described as embryonic, with projects such as the human genome map providing a new language in which to understand human health and disease, the ageing process, and the basic mechanisms of biological reproduction. Similarly, the mapping of the genomes of mice, fruit flies, micro-organisms such as yeast, and higher vertebrates such as dogs and sheep is yielding basic information about the nature of what are commonly described as the genetic instructions for the production of all living things. In turn, this information is being combined with an increasingly complex understanding of the protein pathways which condition genetic expression, and the cellular processes with which they interact, to devise new means of harnessing biological reproduction as a means of manufacture.

Cloning, then, is neither new nor necessarily controversial. Techniques of cloning have been used in agriculture for millennia, and methods such as polymerase chain reaction (PCR), which is a form of cloning widely used in genetic engineering, have been standard and non-controversial procedures for decades. What is new about the method of 'cloning' known as the Dolly technique is its global prominence as a highly publicised and powerfully symbolic marker of an intensification of molecular engineering at the level of the basic biological pathways of organic reproduction. Dolly's status as a world-famous 'clone' is thus most accurately interpreted as a form of symbolic association, which attaches the highly controversial spectre of cloning (itself a term that has long signified cultural anxiety about man-made life) to a significant development in reproductive biology. This association is fully justified, in that the success of the Dolly technique is indeed a very good example of the power of biotechnology to re-engineer living organisms, and of the desires of scientists and commercial industries to increase their abilities to do so. Thus, despite the fact that it is somewhat misleading to describe Dolly as a clone in the technical sense of the term, this term accurately conveys a significant level of public anxiety about the question of limits to scientific manipulation of life itself. Both the many techniques which come under the broad umbrella of cloning, and the wider biotechnological industry of which they are a part, rely on an increasing ability to rewrite the rules of biological reproduction.

CNR and stem cells

In May 1999 the California-based pharmaceutical corporation Geron purchased Ian Wilmut's Dolly division at Roslin for 25.7 million dollars (in stock options), and announced a 20 million dollar research programme over the next 6 years to combine the use of nuclear transfer with Geron's human cell-line technology to create a new market in human tissue replacement therapy, or human therapeutic cloning.

The new company, Geron BioMed, is a wholly owned subsidiary of Geron Corporation, based at Roslin, and is described by its parent company as the world's 'premiere research and development consortium in transplantation biology' (Geron press release, 4 May 1999). The goal of this consortium is to develop novel forms of human cell therapy that combine Geron's expertise in overcoming the cellular ageing process with Roslin's ability to reprogramme adult cells to re-differentiate. In other words, the aim is to provide a kind of bespoke tissue therapy for a wide range of human diseases from heart failure to cancer treatment to Parkinson's disease. This will be accomplished by taking body cells *from the afflicted patient*, turning them into pluripotent[2] cell lines that *act like* early embryonic tissue, which can then be redirected to produce numerous forms of specialised human tissue suitable for re-implantation back into the patient.

The company's most widely publicised research is the ability to clone telomerase, the enzyme which controls the mamallian cellular ageing process. In their own words, Geron's greatest breakthrough has been to 'discover the key to cellular mortality'. This 'key' is Geron's patented telomerase reactivation technology. Telomeres are described by Geron as the finger-like protrusions at the ends of each chromosome (Geron uses the analogy of shoelaces, with their protected tips). Found in all mammalian cells, telomeres act as the 'mitotic clock' of cellular replication by shortening with each cell division. Telomere shortening eventually causes the cessation of cell division, in other words, cell death. However, telomere shortening can be reversed by means of reactivating the enzyme telomerase, which adds DNA repeats to the telomeres as cells divide, thus 'resetting' the cellular clock, and making cells more youthful, or, indeed, immortal.[3]

From Geron's point of view, what is very useful about the Dolly technique is that it enables significant improvements in human cell line technology.[4] Geron's ability to reactivate telomerase within specially cultured cell lines made of human embryonic stem cells offers, in their words, the capacity 'to produce large quantities of perpetually-young and healthy differentiated cells for use in the repair of degenerating organs' (Geron Corporation, 1997).

In 2001 George Bush announced a ban on the creation of any new stem cell lines in the US. Following a personal consultation with the Vatican, and in response to public pressures to ban the use of human embryonic tissue in the manufacturing of cell lines, Bush's restrictions created a less favourable research environment in the US, where stem cell research is most advanced. Meanwhile, stem cell research in Europe has been strongly encouraged by the European Commission, leading some countries, most notably Germany, to liberalise their laws on embryo research to allow them to be used for making cell lines. According to the leading EC scientific research bulletin of 2001, 'Europe seems determined not to miss the stem cell train. The European Union already funds – to the sum of 27.4 million euro – 15 research projects involving 117 laboratories in countries from Finland to Portugal' (European Commission, 2001, p. 7).

Britain has emerged as the leading European country to use the Dolly technique in conjunction with human embryonic cells to manufacture stem cells, and has produced comprehensive legislative guidelines to regulate this field. According to the British House of Lords Select Committee Report on Stem Cell Research, published in February 2002:

> Until recently it has generally been considered that in mammalian cells the process of differentiation is irreversible. However, it has been demonstrated in animals that it is possible to reprogramme ('dedifferentiate') the genetic material of a differentiated adult cell by CNR. Following this seminal finding, many studies have also suggested that adult stem cells may have greater 'plasticity' than previously suspected: they may be reprogrammed to give rise to cell types to which they normally do not give rise in the body. The potential of specialised cells to differentiate into cell types other than those to which they normally give rise in the body is little short of a revolutionary concept in cell biology. It has significantly increased the possibilities for developing effective stem-cell based therapies.
> (House of Lords (HL), 2002, p. 13)

The British House of Lords Report offers a thorough consideration of stem cell research and concludes it should be 'strongly encouraged by funding bodies and the Government' in Britain (HL, 2002, p. 48). Research on human embryos is described as 'necessary, particularly to understand the processes of cell differentiation and dedifferentiation' and the Report endorses the CNR technique, stating that 'there is a powerful case for its use . . . as a research tool to enable other cell-based therapies to be developed' (pp. 48–9). The report recommends the establishment of a British stem cell bank to be 'responsible for the custody of stem cell lines, ensuring their purity and provenance' (p. 50) and concludes that existing mechanisms for regulation of research, and mechanisms for procuring informed consent from donors, are sufficiently robust to accommodate new developments in the area of stem cell research.

Although the House of Lords Committee acknowledges that they were only able to give limited attention to the role of commercial interests in stem cell research, it devotes an entire section of its report to this concern and acknowledges it has 'been aware throughout that commercial interests could, and to some extent already do, play an important role in the development of such research' (HL, 2002, p. 32). It is also acknowledged that 'biotechnology is a growth industry', citing an Ernst & Young report that by the end of 2000 'the total value of Europe's publicly quoted biotechnology companies stood at 75 billion Euros, compared with 36 billion Euros a year earlier' (HL, 2002, p. 32).

These references, along with acknowledgement that the United Kingdom 'has by far the most public biotechnology companies' in Europe, and that 'investor interest is considerable and evidently based on the assumption that future profits may be significant', confirm the extent to which the British government recognises the importance of economic growth in the biotechnology sector as a national priority. This is further underlined by reference in the House of Lords report to China and Singapore, which 'provide examples that deserve special mention':

> In China the government has encouraged a number of universities to invest heavily in stem cell research. In doing so universities have attracted not only public funds but investment by private companies like the Beijing Stemcell Medengineering Company. Leading Chinese researchers are often US-trained and have links with American laboratories. In Singapore, the Economic Development Board has provided initial finance for the Singapore genetics Programme; it is said that by 2005 some \$7 billion dollars will have been invested in relevant research. In both China and Singapore there is concern with ethical issues but also an interest to maintain the competitive advantage gained by light regulation.
>
> (HL, 2002, p. 32)

In March of 2002, shortly following publication of the House of Lords Report, and following the approval of the first licences for stem cell research using human embryos in Britain, one of the world's leading stem cell scientists, Austin Smith of the Centre for Human Genome Research in Edinburgh, published an article in *Nature* suggesting that much of the work conducted on stem cells may have misidentified their properties. Cells which were thought to have been 'reprogrammed', or 'de-differentiated', may, his study suggested, have simply merged with other cells to produce cell populations with a double set of chromosomes (Terada *et al.*, 2002, and Ying *et al.*, 2002). Smith claims it took the better part of two decades to stabilise and characterise murine cell lines, and that it is likely that human embryonic cell lines may be similarly time-consuming to establish. Such claims, although they counter much of the hype that has surrounded human therapeutic cloning and stem cells, point towards their eventual use, albeit possibly as a more distant option than was once hoped.

Conclusion

The development of cloning by nuclear transfer, now known as CNR or 'the Dolly technique', has undergone several transformations since its inaugural use as a form of animal breeding in a livestock research facility in the mid-1990s. Amidst ongoing unconfirmed reports in the early twenty-first century that several women may already be pregnant with cloned offspring, a human has so far not been born who has been scientifically proven to have been cloned. Human reproductive cloning is widely considered to be unethical, due to the high incidence of congenital abnormality in all known cloned vertebrates, and has been denounced by all but a few maverick practitioners, such as the Italian clinician Severino Antinori. Use of the Dolly technique for the production of stem cells, and for what has come to be known as the field of regenerative medicine, has, in contrast, launched one of the first major post-genomic bio-industries. Stem cell research using CNR, which is often described as tissue engineering, has become a major research focus in Europe, and continues to be a high priority area for many US biotechnology companies, such as Associated Cell Technologies, based in Worcester, Massachusetts, which is the leading US competitor to the Geron corporation. China and Singapore also have burgeoning stem cell industries which receive significant public assistance, in what has become one of the most competitive global biotechnology sectors.

It is likely that the future of 'cloning' will lie primarily in the petri dish, although it is certain also to occupy a prominent position in the media, in popular culture and in academic debate. It is claimed by many to be one of the most significant developments in twentieth century biology, and is likely to play a leading role in the formation of health-care strategies in the future, along with pharmacogenetics and genetic screening technologies. It will, in all of these capacities, continue to pose unique challenges at the level of governance and regulation, as well as in the effort to maintain public trust towards the genomic sciences as they permeate ever more deeply into definitions of human identity, health and reproduction.

Notes

1 See further at the PPL Therapeutics website, www.ppl-therapeutics.co.uk.
2 The useful feature of early embryonic cells is their ability to retain the capacity to differentiate into any kind of tissue: so-called 'totipotentiality'. Geron distinguishes between their 'pluripotent' cell lines, which can become most, but not all, forms of tissue (for example, they cannot, at present, be directed to become blood cells), and the 'true' totipotential capacities of early embryos.
3 Like early embryonic cells, cancer cells do not lose their telomeres, which is why cancer cells are commonly used to establish immortal cell lines. Initially, Geron aimed for a market in diagnostic kits which would test for telomerase to identify oncogenesis. This is still an important emerging market for Geron, though somewhat displaced by the new avenues made possible through using nuclear transfer to make better immortal ('more immortal') cell lines.
4 A normal cell line made from body tissue has to be mixed with several other ingredients, many of unknown function, in order to activate and become productive. Making a cell line of, for example, the mammary tissue of a Finn Dorset ewe requires a complicated cocktail of ingredients to achieve a small fibroblast, as the resulting scab-like collection of mammary cells in culture has many needs that are not well understood.

References

European Commission (2001) 'Stem cells: promises and precautions', *RTD Info*, 32: 3–9, Brussels.
Franklin, S. (1999) '"Orphaned" Embryos', in Edwards, J., Franklin, S., Hirsch, E., Price, F., Strathern, M. (eds) *Technologies of Procreation: kinship in the age of assisted conception*, 2nd Edition, Routledge, London, pp. 166–70.
House of Lords (2002) *Stem Cell Research*, HMSO, London.
Lovell-Badge, R. (2001) 'The future for stem cell research', *Nature*, 414, pp. 88–91, 1 November.
Silver, L. (1999) *Remaking Eden: cloning, genetic engineering and the future of humankind?*, Phoenix, London.
Terada, N., Hamazaki, T., Oka, M., Hoki, M., Mastalerz, D. M., Nakano, Y., Meyer, E. M., Morel, L., Petersen, B. E. and Scott, E. W. (2002) 'Bone marrow cells adopt phenotype of other cells by spontaneous cell fusion', *Nature*, Advanced online publication DOI: nature 730.
Ying, O. L., Nichols, J., Evans, E. and Smith, A. G. (2002) 'Changing potency by spontaneous fusion', *Nature*, Advanced online publication DOI: nature 729.

Further reading

Keller, Evelyn Fox (2000) *The Century of the Gene*, Cambridge, MA: Harvard University Press.
Kolata, Gina (1997) *Clone: the road to Dolly and the path ahead*, London, Allen Lane.
Nussbaum, Martha C. and Sunstein, Cass R. (1998) *Clones and Clones: facts and fantasies about human cloning*, New York, W.W. Norton.
Wilmut, Ian, Campbell, Keith and Tudge, Colin (2000) *The Second Creation: the age of biological control by the scientists who cloned Dolly*, London, Headline.

Biography

Sarah Franklin is Professor of Anthropology of Science at Lancaster University. In addition to numerous articles and chapters on cloning and reproductive technology, she is the author of *Embodied Progress: a cultural account of assisted conception* (1997) and co-author of *Technologies of Procreation: kinship in the age of assisted conception* (1999) and *Global Nature, Global Culture* (2000). Her co-edited anthologies include *Reproducing Reproduction: kinship, power and technological innovation* (1998) and *Relative Values: reconfiguring kinship studies* (2001). She is currently completing a book about cloning entitled *Dolly Mixtures*.

Part III
In vitro fertilisation

8   *In vitro* fertilisation

Only for the infertile?

Juliet Tizzard

In vitro fertilisation (IVF) has been with us for nearly a quarter of a century and has led to the birth of over a million so-called test tube babies world-wide. Yet, despite its transition from an experimental to a routine medical intervention, it continues to attract just as much public and media attention as it did in the late 1970s. The public discussion about IVF has changed over the years, from debates in the early days about the moral status of human embryos to more recent, additional concerns about who gets access to IVF and why.

IVF and embryo research: the ethical issues

Human fertilisation, of course, normally takes place inside the body, out of the sight of doctors, scientists and even the prospective parents. IVF departs from this norm by making fertilisation happen in a laboratory, but its intervention in the natural process is very short-lived, since the resulting embryo is placed in the womb within two or three days. Thus, in IVF the embryo has spent a tiny fraction of the nine months of development from conception to birth in what might be considered an unnatural environment. But does this change of location, at what is obviously a crucial time, make any ethical difference?

Bringing about conception in a petri dish is certainly strange (and it must have seemed very strange in the very early days of IVF), but those who are concerned about or even unequivocally opposed to IVF are not concerned so much about where conception is taking place. Instead, what they usually object to is that in IVF, whilst some embryos are transferred to the womb in the hope of a pregnancy, many others are destroyed.

In order to maximise the chance of a successful conception, women undergoing IVF treatment are given drugs to make them produce more than the usual one egg per month: usually between five and ten eggs are stimulated to grow in the ovary. These are collected and fertilised by sperm in a petri dish, hopefully resulting in the production of a number of embryos for possible transfer to the patient. Having more than one embryo available for transfer increases the chance of a successful conception in three ways. First, by having a number of embryos in the laboratory, the embryologist can choose those which look most likely to implant in the womb and grow. Second, if two or three embryos are transferred, the woman has a better chance of becoming pregnant in that cycle than if just one had been transferred. The final advantage of creating more than one embryo in the laboratory is that any left over after embryo transfer can be frozen for potential use at a later date. This means that the woman could have more embryos transferred in future IVF cycles without having to undergo again the ovarian stimulation drug regimen and the egg collection.

This ability to create and store surplus embryos means that IVF is a far more successful treatment than it might otherwise be. But it also means that some of these embryos will die or be destroyed. The person or couple undergoing treatment might not wish to store the embryos or they might store them and then decide later that they do not wish to use them. In either case, they can ask for the embryos to be destroyed or they can ask for them to be given to research after which they will be destroyed. In the United Kingdom, under the Human Fertilisation and Embryology (HFE) Act 1990, human embryos can be kept in frozen storage for a maximum of five years, after which time they must be used or destroyed.[1]

Some people find this embryo destruction unacceptable because they think that human life should be protected from the moment of conception. For them, the human embryo may have a moral status which is equal to that of any fetus, child or adult. Whilst the debate about the moral status of the human embryo was an important one in the early days of IVF and still has relevance today, most people take the view that the creation of human embryos outside the body and the inevitable loss of some of them is a price worth paying in the quest to help the infertile have children.

Two practical drawbacks of IVF are its cost and its relative lack of success. IVF is an expensive business – largely because of the drug regimens involved – costing thousands of pounds each time it is attempted. In the UK most people undergoing treatment have to bear this cost themselves, as the National Health Service pays for only about 10% of IVF cycles. Added to the financial burden is the low chance of success of treatment. Latest statistics show that 18% of treatment cycles started lead to the birth of a live baby.[2] However, this should be compared with the chance of conception in a fertile couple, which is roughly 25% in each monthly cycle.

IVF for the fertile?

Although IVF was originally developed to help women with blocked Fallopian tubes become pregnant, its actual and potential applications have widened enormously over its twenty-five year history. In the early days many people feared that IVF would soon become the method of choice for having children; that natural conception would go out of favour in the face of new, 'sex-free' ways of conceiving. Whilst these rather doom-laden visions of the future failed to materialise, the scope of IVF has broadened, leading to a situation where those who are not necessarily infertile can use the technique to have children.

Such people have often been referred to as socially infertile: those who, because of certain life choices they have made, are unable or unwilling to use natural conception to have children. They include single women who wish to become a single parent; men or women in same-sex relationships; women who wish to delay motherhood until later in their reproductive lives (in their forties or early fifties, for instance) and those who wish to have a child after the menopause. All these people are unable to have children naturally not because of any medical problem – such as blocked Fallopian tubes or the failure to produce enough good quality sperm – but because natural conception is not for them, because they want to have a child either outside a heterosexual relationship or outside the time-frame that nature normally allows.

The issues mentioned above usually provide the material for public and media discussion about IVF today. Gone are the days when the moral status of human embryos was the only subject of popular debate about IVF. Now it is issues relating to access to IVF – who gets it and for what purposes – which test our moral sensibilities.

How can we assess the ethical implications of such uses of IVF technologies? One approach is to ask whether the types of families which reproductive tech-nologies can create are fundamentally different from families created by the natural methods that we know and accept. If, for example, a lesbian couple can have children without medical intervention, for example with a male friend, and if we don't seek to prevent this, then the case against preventing the creation of such families by assisted conception is considerably weakened. A lesbian couple, after all, might prefer to find their own sperm donor in order to achieve a pregnancy, or they could approach a fertility clinic where donors are anonymous and have no parental rights over the resulting child.[3]

If some families *cannot* be created by natural means (such as those where the mother has passed the menopause), then we must ask whether they are proble-matic, particularly in relation to the welfare of the children in comparison to the welfare of children born to more traditional families. If, alternatively, similar families *can* be created by natural means but we remain uneasy about using reproductive technology to create them, we must find a compelling reason why IVF is worthy of special status. Is there anything about creating families through IVF which shifts the ethical goalposts?

Single women

Sometimes women find that by the time they start wanting children they haven't found the right male partner with whom to have them. Other women feel that they'd rather not have a partner at all and would prefer to go it alone as a parent. For whatever reason a woman finds herself on her own and wanting a child, she could use sperm from a fertility clinic in order to achieve a pregnancy. No IVF treatment is required: it is a simple case of syringing sperm into the woman without having to create embryos outside the body. However, such services are often provided through IVF by fertility clinics and have the attendant advantage of guaranteeing the medical screening (for HIV or genetic diseases, for instance) of sperm donors and, assuming this is what the woman prefers, the donor's anonymity and lack of parental responsibility. Such sperm donation services offer single women the opportunity to become mothers without any involvement (apart from the provision of sperm) from a man.

Two concerns about single women becoming mothers in this way have been voiced. The first is that medical services are being used to remove men from the parenting process. Following on from this, the second concern is that the removal of a man from the family unit is damaging to the resulting child. The most obvious rebuttal of the first concern is that these women do not necessarily need the assistance of a fertility clinic to become a mother. They could make a private arrangement with a friend or even have sex with someone without telling them about their intention to conceive. Given that society, even if we so desired, cannot intervene in such private activities, it seems unjust to seek to prevent a woman going to a sperm bank to bring about the same outcome by what is a safer and possibly more honest method.

What about the absence of a father? Is it necessarily detrimental to a child to grow up without any male influence in their lives? It is often suggested that children who grow up in one-parent families may be more disadvantaged educationally and psychologically than those in two-parent families. But, as Golombok observes,[4] this may be caused more by financial hardship, divorce or other problems associated with one-parent families than by the lack of a father in itself. Lee and Morgan note that one in eight families in the UK are one-parent families, the vast majority of which start out as two-parent families. They go on to ask: 'Does it make any sense to suppose that the social and emotional development of . . . IVF children in fatherless families would be different from that of children who find themselves in heterosexual one-parent families . . . after they reach the age of two or three years?'[5]

Same-sex couples

The prospect of same-sex couples using IVF to become parents has provoked both similar and additional concerns to those raised by single women becoming mothers. Although children born into these families will have two parents, they lack a social father (in the case of a lesbian couple) or a social mother (in the case of a gay couple). Is this cause for concern?

In the case of a lesbian couple, the woman who is to be the biological mother is in almost exactly the same position as the single woman discussed above. She doesn't necessarily need medical intervention and could make a private arrangement instead, so seeking to prevent her use of donor sperm in a fertility clinic seems unfair. Unlike the single woman, however, this woman has a partner and is, arguably, able to provide a more stable family environment with two parents in a loving relationship.

IVF has been used by gay couples wishing to become parents to a child born of different biological and gestational mothers. In the case of Tony Barlow and Barrie Drewitt, which hit the headlines in the UK in September 1999,[6] a donor egg was used, which was fertilised by one of the men and then transferred to the womb of a surrogate mother. However, two men becoming parents is not dependent upon IVF technology. A couple could make a private arrangement with a surrogate, who would be the biological mother as well as the gestational mother of the child. But however the conception is brought about, a child born to a gay couple still has two parents, albeit of the same sex.

What about the impact upon the child? There is very little research on the psychological impact on children when they have been born to same-sex parents using sperm or egg donation and surrogacy. However, Golombok argues that children growing up in families where the parents are of the same sex – regardless of *how* they were conceived – seem to fare just as well as their friends with heterosexual parents. Whilst there may still be some stigma attached to having gay parents, this does not seem to impair the child psychologically or educationally.

Delayed and post-menopausal motherhood

Since the advent of embryo freezing in 1984 IVF technology can be used to delay parenthood whilst maximising the chance of conception. Although most use of embryo freezing is for the medically infertile who wish to freeze their embryos for a short period of time between IVF cycles or for those who risk infertility by being exposed to treatments such as chemotherapy, a small but growing number of people are seeking to use freezing technology to delay parenthood for non-medical reasons. These include couples who wish to freeze embryos created early in their reproductive lives for use later on and single women who wish to freeze their eggs for fertilisation later, either when they have found a partner or when they wish to have a child.

For these people, the use of freezing technology enables them to extend their fertile years to a time when, although they might be able to conceive naturally, the likelihood of their being able to do so is significantly reduced. The ability of women to conceive naturally falls rapidly after the age of about 35 years. In this context, freezing – whether of eggs or embryos – is a kind of insurance policy against the realities of nature. But since they *could* conceive naturally, even in their late forties, it seems unjust to prevent their use of freezing technology in order to do the same with more chance of success.

Some women leave it too late to conceive with their own eggs and reach the menopause still wanting to become a mother. In the past their desires would be frustrated by the limits of nature. But the advent of IVF and egg donation meant that, for the first time, post-menopausal women could conceive and carry a pregnancy to term. However, despite its rarity, there has been considerable opposition to postmenopausal motherhood and to the doctors who make it possible. Lynn Bezant, whose pregnancy at the age of 56 years became public

knowledge in January 2001, was heavily criticised for opting for postmenopausal motherhood. One fertility specialist echoed a widely held view that
'elderly parents are not considered to be in the best interest of the child'.[7]

A number of objections to postmenopausal motherhood have been raised.
The first is that it is impossible to achieve without IVF and egg donation.
No natural processes are restored, because postmenopausal women would
never normally be able to conceive. Some people feel that such women
should not expect to 'have it all' and should respect the limits that nature,
quite sensibly, imposes. Another concern is for the child: with a mother perhaps
55 years its senior, will the child suffer from having a parent who is lacking in
energy and who, more importantly, might not live long enough to see it into
adulthood?

It is certainly true that without IVF and egg donation, postmenopausal
motherhood would not be possible. But that does not necessarily make it
wrong (without aeroplanes, for instance, air travel would be impossible, but
no-one considers it to be wrong for that reason). Some say that the menopause
is an appropriate, naturally imposed limit which rightly prevents women who
are simply too old to have children from having them. However, death is
also a naturally imposed limit, but not one which we unquestioningly respect.
Furthermore, whilst older women face a higher risk of complications during
pregnancy and childbirth, it is still quite possible for a woman in her sixties
to carry a pregnancy and give birth without harm to herself or the baby.

What about the effect upon the child and the fact that it might lose its mother
at a relatively young age? This is certainly a major consideration for anyone
thinking about starting a family later in life, but is it a reason to forbid them
from doing so? Whilst we might have private reservations, we wouldn't prevent
someone with a shortened life expectancy (someone who knows they will
develop Huntington's disease, for instance) from having children. Society
trusts such individuals to have thought through their decision and to have
made adequate provisions for their children in the event of death.

Is there anything special about IVF?

We have seen that some social uses of reproductive technology to create families
do not differ greatly from natural methods of conception. Medical assistance,
rather than making the impossible possible, is sought because it offers a greater
chance of success, safety, confidentiality and, perhaps, peace of mind. There is
little justification for preventing these people from accessing assisted conception
services to have a family which would be possible without them. In fact, given
the potential advantages of using assisted conception services, it could be argued
that such people should be encouraged, rather than discouraged, from using
them.

Others, such as postmenopausal women, seek to create families which would
not be possible without the assistance of reproductive medicine. Some have
argued that the question of whether or not the creation of such families is

possible without medical intervention is irrelevant. What matters is that assisted conception, unlike natural conception, requires the involvement of one or more medical professionals and that this involvement has a moral dimension. Many argue that this moral dimension even extends to a responsibility to refuse treatment to those whom that doctor considers to be unfit for parenthood. In short, the doctor has a moral responsibility to the potential child.

In the UK the Human Fertilisation and Embryology Act places a legal responsibility upon IVF clinicians to take account of 'the welfare of any child who may be born as a result of the treatment'.[8] If a clinician believes that the welfare of any child born to a particular woman or couple requesting treatment will be compromised, he or she must refuse access to treatment. However, there is very little guidance on how this paragraph should be interpreted, the result being that each clinic has a different policy on what types of requests for treatment they accede to.

Regardless of how this 'welfare of the child' paragraph should be interpreted, a clinician in the UK clearly does have some degree of responsibility to the potential child. But does this make sense? Do IVF doctors have a moral (quite apart from a legal) responsibility for the children they help to create? As we have seen, the involvement of these doctors in the baby-making process is rather fleeting, albeit crucial. The doctor has had no involvement in the decision to try for a baby in the first place and will have no further involvement with the couple once the baby is born. It could be argued that the decision (whether, when and how) to have a child and how one brings up that child are the two most important stages of the child-rearing process. The conception stage in between, whilst pivotal, is little more than a technical step which makes the transition from childlessness to parenthood possible. To imbue this technical involvement with a moral dimension not only serves to overestimate the doctor's importance in the process, but it also serves to underplay the prospective parents' responsibility in having and caring for a child.

If doctors have a moral responsibility, it is a duty to act in the best interests of their patient: the woman or couple requesting treatment. Those best interests are better served by allowing patients the autonomy to make important parental decisions themselves rather then attempting to make those decisions on their behalf.

Notes

1 Human Fertilisation and Embryology Act 1990, section 14(4), as amended by the Human Fertilisation and Embryology (Statutory Storage Period for Embryos) Regulations 1996 (SI 1996 No. 375).
2 Human Fertilisation and Embryology Authority Annual Report 2000.
3 Human Fertilisation and Embryology Act 1990, section 28.
4 Susan Golombok, *Parenting: what really counts?* London, Routledge, 2001.
5 Robert G. Lee and Derek Morgan, *Human Fertilisation and Embryology: regulating the reproductive revolution*, Blackstone Press, 2001.
6 'Gay couple pay for surrogate mother's twins', *Guardian*, 2 September 1999.

7 'Specialist supports rights of mum-to-be', *Independent*, 23 January 2001.
8 Human Fertilisation and Embryology Act 1990, section 13(5).

Further reading

For insights into the psychological impact of new reproductive technologies on the offspring, see Susan Golombok, *Parenting: what really counts?* (Routledge, 2001).

For legal and ethical analysis of reproductive technologies, see: Robert G. Lee and Derek Morgan, *Human Fertilisation and Embryology: regulating the reproductive revolution* (Blackstone Press, 2001); Emily Jackson, *Regulating Reproduction: law, technology and autonomy* (Hart Publishing, 2001); John Harris and Søren Holm, *The Future of Human Reproduction* (Clarendon Press, 1998).

For news stories and ethical analysis of developments in reproductive technology and associated research, see *BioNews*, published by Progress Educational Trust, at www.BioNews.org.uk.

Biography

Juliet Tizzard is director of Progress Educational Trust, a charity set up to promote the benefits of reproductive and genetic science. She is also editor-in-chief of BioNews.org.uk, a web-based news and comment service, also on reproductive and genetic science. A graduate of Kings College London's MA in Medical Law and Ethics, Juliet has written on a range of bioethical issues.

9 Surrogacy

A case study in ethics[1]

Marilyn Strathern

It is a truism about technological innovation that science and technology race ahead while society and its views lag behind, never quite catching up. This is particularly so of ethics. What one Berkshire Post Office worker said more than a decade ago still holds:

> Medicine is racing well ahead; do we morally feel we are in agreement with what they're doing? We probably need time to catch up the medical people . . . I suppose, given enough time, we will all start to think differently.
>
> (Hirsch, 1999: 118, emphasis removed)

In the background at that time was the Human Fertilisation and Embryology Act, 1990, and the debates it generated in the press and elsewhere. The Act was envisaged as working out some kind of relationship between technology and society. As a pharmacist from the same suburb observed to the enquiring anthropologist (Hirsch, 1999: 116): 'Lots of things are [technically] possible now, it's just that they wouldn't morally be accepted.'

The inevitability of scientific progress was an issue for many in both the Commons and the Lords debates at the time (see Franklin, 1999). The principal ethical view that framed the original Committee of Inquiry under Mary Warnock in 1984, established to look at the new medical possibilities in human fertilisation and early development raised by the new technique of *in vitro* fertilisation, was that there had to be barriers of some kind to scientific 'progress'. Such a wish for limits was seen to rest with people in general.

> What is common . . . is that people generally want *some principles or other* to govern the development and use of the new techniques. There must be *some* barriers that are not to be crossed. . . . The very existence of morality depends on it. . . . In recognising that there should be limits, people are bearing witness to the existence of a moral ideal of society.
>
> (Warnock, 1985: 2, original emphasis)

Several years later we are grappling with problems that were then at the outer limits of people's imagining, of which 'cloning' is a prime example. Take an application of 'cloning' known today as stem-cell therapy: the UK Parliament (2001–2) has been debating the ethics of research in this area precisely because the technology has 'raced well ahead' of the provisions of the 1990 Act.

But some things have been settled. It is interesting therefore to consider an instance where an ethical judgement has endured. It comes from the late 1980s/early 1990s. The judgement was made by ordinary people, not by anyone in particular but just in the way that certain words have acquired certain meanings and have stuck. Indeed, it is so embedded in the way people talk that you probably would not notice it. I refer to the terms we use for surrogate mothers.

Different kinds of surrogacy

One medical advance that stimulated the 1990 Act was the possibility of fertilised eggs ('embryos') living outside the womb; this in turn led to improved implantation procedures so that the egg might be returned not to the woman who had ovulated but to another woman altogether. A new kind of maternal surrogacy emerged,[2] which took advantage of this innovation.

Procedures such as *in vitro* fertilisation and embryo transfer made it possible to separate procreation from gestation. This gave rise to all kinds of possibilities for infertile couples. It included the possibility of finding substitutes not just for parental genetic material but for the womb. The nub of surrogacy agreements, as they came to be called, was the intention of a woman gestating an embryo/fetus to hand the child when it was born over to other persons, preferably a couple. *New technologies demand new social practices – new social relationships are brought into being.* The intending parents of the child to be were known as the commissioning parents. My interest is in how some of the relationships are perceived.

Nowadays the complexities of the relationships arising from *in vitro* fertilisation and surrogacy are sometimes very considerable. For example, there have been cases where the woman gestating the embryo is the mother of the woman whose egg gave rise to the foetus. There are also many cases where the sperm used to fertilise the egg comes not from the partner of the woman who provides the egg but from another man. This is typically because the male partner of the woman who provides the egg is infertile but also occurs when a lesbian couple have a baby by surrogacy. Here, though, the intention is more straightforwardly to explore how relationships came to be understood in the simpler case where there is no genetic relatedness between the two women and where the sperm comes from the male partner of the woman who ends up (with her partner) looking after the baby.

For a period there was considerable fluidity around the designations of the various parties. Early on a contrast was established between partial and full surrogacy, between contributing both uterus and egg and contributing the uterus alone. In the USA the former was also called 'traditional' surrogacy, and the latter 'host' or 'gestational' surrogacy. With technological improvements and increasing demand, gestational surrogacy became more widespread, and the designation became common usage in English. Most surrogacy arangements today are of this kind.

The *New Dictionary of Medical Ethics* (Boyd, Higgs and Pinching, 1997) defines the surrogate as follows: 'the use of a third party to assist a couple in conceiving and bearing a child when the commissioning woman is either lacking a uterus or is unable to use her own uterus for medical reasons'. However, if we go back to when surrogacy was being debated in the British parliament, we find a specialist in health-care law noting just the opposite definition:

> By surrogacy. . . I mean an understanding or agreement by which a woman – the surrogate mother – agrees to bear a child for another person or couple. Of course *this popular understanding* immediately encounters the objection that it is the person . . . who takes and rears the child rather than she who gives birth who is properly the surrogate. The woman giving birth [should be regarded as] the mother.
> (Morgan 1989: 56, my emphasis; author's emphasis removed)

The objection came from those who took the view of the English law of the period, namely that the woman who bore the child was the child's legal mother, and her husband the child's legal father. (Intending parents could make a case for adoption if, among other conditions, the child were genetically related to at least one of them.) The objection was that in popular understandings parenthood had become defined as 'genetic' and was ignoring the authenticity of the gestational and therefore birth mother.

Now, taken separately, ordinary definitions of the English term 'mother' (woman who has given birth) and 'surrogate' (one who acts in the place of another) would seem to support the objection. The surrogate would be the woman who subsequently acquires a child which another has borne. But the reverse view, which the *Dictionary* encoded, was not to be dislodged. For popular usage was determined to have it the other way round. It was the term surrogate which became irrevocably and stubbornly tied to the woman who in these circumstances bears the child. I am going to suggest that beyond the genetic issue there were other reasons for that stubbornness. It endorsed an ethical view on a social relationship at the heart of these new techniques.

The ethics of relationship

The figure of the surrogate mother (in gestational arrangements) makes explicit a connection between gestation and other factors in childbirth. The meaning of surrogacy is thus established *in relation* to a common understanding of motherhood. Now gestation on the part of the birth mother may be interpreted as 'more' or 'less' biological and as 'more' or 'less' indicative of authentic mother-hood, depending on the context. It itself is not diagnostic of surrogacy. The diagnostic issue is that one woman is perceived to be carrying a child for another woman.[3] She represents an aspect of motherhood but is not otherwise the mother. She is a stand-in, occupying the place of the mother for a while, discharging an important function, but always in reference to another person who by implication is the eventual parent. It is precisely because she stands in for that element that otherwise defines motherhood that she is the surrogate. Popular English usage was certain on this.

Relations between aspects of motherhood translate into relationships between persons. Note that the arrangements depend on the agreement of the gestational surrogate to bear the child for the commissioning couple, not of the commissioning couple to rear the child for the birth mother. To the ordinary person, the intentions underlying the relationship are clear. Contest only arises when *the relationship* between the surrogate and the woman on whose behalf she is bearing the child breaks down. When gestation is claimed to be definitive of her own motherhood, the surrogate is no longer a surrogate.

However, this is not how people generally talk about surrogacy. They cut through the issues with a very simple device: distinguishing between the mothers. The surrogate is not, by definition, the 'real' mother. This piece of popular wisdom remained a point of clarity amid all the questions that con-tinued to be asked about the apparent doubling of the maternal contribution. But everything depended on the surrogate remaining willing to keep that relationship going.

Altruism and selfishness

The surrogate role is quite straightforward: one person stands in for another. The designation points to the fact that the real mother must be another person than herself. Surrogacy thus belongs to the world of agreements and contracts between persons by contrast with the 'real' or 'natural' motherhood, which is established by an appeal to some inherent characteristic, for example the wish or intention, the 'biological drive', to be a parent.

This was acted out in legal disputes at the time, and they were much publi-cised,[4] where a woman who agreed to act as a gestational surrogate then wished to claim the child as hers, that is, made a claim to be the real mother. In other words, the stand-in claimed she was not a stand-in after all. Here one claim *substitutes* for another.

What do I mean by substitute? The difference is between 'standing in' for another and 'taking the place of' another. The former requires sustaining a relationship between the two 'mothers' (even if limited to the period of gesta-tion), the latter supplanting and denying it. In short, the difference is no more nor less than *the visibility of the relationship between them* (the two women).[5] The 'surrogate mother' is a surrogate as long as her relationship with the 'other' mother is intact; should she claim the child to be 'hers', however, she then substitutes for that other woman. For to desire to be a mother is generally taken as requiring no further justification. When the surrogate instead substitutes her own maternal impulse (to have a child) for altruism (to bear a child for another) this is understandable; indeed the generosity perceived in the act is generally approved. Surrogate mother, 'real' altruist.

If it is the relationship between the two mothers which guarantees that the commissioning mother will in the end receive the child of her desires, the same relationship also keeps the surrogate mother's acts morally acceptable. Take it away and the intention of her actions may be thrown into doubt. For her very willingness to act as a surrogate may already carry a substitutive possibility of another kind. In the place of a desire to help there may instead be a desire for money. When the surrogate substitutes a commercial impulse for a maternal one, it too may be understandable but is invariably put into a negative light. Even if she still intends to hand over the child, her altruism is eclipsed by commerce. Perhaps some of the equivocations surrounding the commercial possibilities of surrogacy arrangements turn on the substitutive and thus displacement effect that money introduces. Surrogate mother, 'real' profiteer.

In the UK the 1990 Act was intended to set up, as it did, a licensing authority for certain treatments of infertility and associated embryo research. While the government's position was that both treatment and research should be encouraged, it drew back from allowing the market to intervene as a mechanism for regulating supply and demand. An explicit provision in the Act debarred the donors of gametes from being able to profit from the donation (S12(e)), and persons who wished to seek an order to be treated as parents of a child from either donated gametes or a surrogacy arrangement could not do so if money had changed hands (S30(7)). The commercialisation of surrogacy by third parties already involved a criminal offence.[6] Whatever the range of needs, surrogacy arrangements were only permissible on a private basis. In the background was the idea that only a private, and thus familial rather than commercial, context would sustain the value of altruism that made the agreement between surrogate and commissioning mother socially acceptable. In seeking money, of course, it was assumed that the surrogate was primarily interested in that and not in the relationship between herself and the other mother.

In other words, the altruism (if only minimally the altruism sealed in a contract) that otherwise justified surrogacy could be displaced by intentions which then appeared as 'the real thing'. Here motherhood and commerce were alternatives.

An analogy

The very term 'surrogacy', I have been suggesting, encapsulates an ethical judgement about the conditions (limits) under which certain acts appear acceptable to others. Altruism is a heavily loaded and positively charged concept, even as commerce or commodification in this arena carries a strong negative charge. Something of that positive charge also adheres to the very idea of a 'relationship', so that we can in English talk of the substitute mother (who wishes to be the 'real' mother and keep the child) as denying relationship (with the commissioning mother). Towards other parties such denial may itself be regarded as a source of altruism, as one member of the public in Lancashire observed: gamete donors who help others without thought of connection with the child act ethically without creating the 'moral ties' that would lead to claims (Edwards, 2000: 228). These diverse relationships between persons give us analogies for relations between different ways of thinking about technology and society.

Reproductive technologies are regarded as facilitating biological process, above all as 'assisting' conception (e.g. Franklin, 1999: 135–6). (They do not assist nurture or those after-birth body processes some have regarded as equally biological in nature.) Such techniques focus on the fertile union of male and female gametes and on the viability of the embryo. In this, artificial insemination, *in vitro* fertilisation and other practices simply *stand in*, so the justification goes, for natural body processes. Not themselves natural, they make up for natural impairment in the same way as the woman who acts on behalf of another's motherhood is a surrogate for her capacity to bear a child. We could consider them surrogate processes.

What makes a surrogate mother like a mother yet not the real mother is the fact that she assists the real mother to overcome impairment. While her gestation of the child is a complete substitute for the commissioning mother's role in gestation, by itself it is an incomplete act that only makes sense when seen as part of the total process by which the real mother is created. (If there were no 'real' mother to receive the child, her act by itself would be meaningless.) In the same way, medical technology is like the natural processes it assists yet is not the natural process itself. Technological intervention helps effect the developmental sequence that creates a child; yet each act of assistance is only given meaning by a successful outcome that is simultaneously a natural one – an egg is fertilised, a child is born. (If there were no encompassing 'natural process', the interventions would have no worthwhile outcome.)

This nudges us to understand another piece of common parlance. A local travel agent told Hirsch (1999: 102) that as long as technology is simply 'giving Nature a helping hand', that's fine; 'fiddling around with the genetics', however, that's wrong. The contrast is between the surrogate technology which sustains a beneficiary relationship with society, and a technology that substitutes its own ends for those of society. But the example ('genetic fiddling'), which comes from 1990, already feels dated.

Notes

1 A version of a talk given to the European Molecular Biology Laboratory, Heidelberg, 1998, in the *Science and Society lecture series*, adapted from Strathern (1998).
2 An 'old' concept (one woman having a child for another) re-made anew through technology.

3 The Glover Report (1989: 67) captures it: 'The term "surrogate" implies that one woman replaces another in her role as mother', although as we shall see there is a critical difference between two modes of 'replacement'. Note that the Warnock Report (1985: 42) was also clear ('Surrogacy is the practice whereby one woman carries a child for another with the intention that the child should be handed over after birth') *until* the possibility of the carrying mother not being the genetic mother arose. This could lead to argument 'as to whether the genetic mother or the carrying mother ought *in truth* to be regarded as the mother of the child' (1985: 44, my emphasis).

4 Primarily in the period leading up to the 1990 Act, see for example Morgan (1989); Wolfram (1989). Commentary continued to pour in from the USA, and stories cirulated widely in the British press.

5 Although the issues fall outside the present argument, we may note that many commentators see the surrogate's relationship with the commissioning mother spelled out in the 'contract' between them – the original agreement by which the former promised to bear a child for the latter. The collapse of the relationship is signalled in the 'breaking' of the contract.

6 The one piece of legislation stemming immediately from the 1984 Warnock Report was the 1985 Surrogacy Arrangements Act, which banned commercial surrogacy.

References

Boyd, Kenneth, Higgs, Roger and Pinching, Anthony (1997) *The New Dictionary of Medical Ethics*, London: BMJ Publishing group.

Edwards, Jeanette (2000) *Born and Bred: idioms of kinsip and new reproductive technologies in England*, Oxford: Oxford University Press.

Franklin, Sarah (1999) [1993] Making representations: the parliamentary debate on the Human Fertilisation and Embryology Act, in Jeanette Edwards, Sarah Franklin, Eric Hirsch, Frances Price and Marilyn Strathern (eds) *Technologies of procreation: Kinship in the age of assisted conception*, 2nd edition, London: Routledge.

Glover, Jonathan (1989) *Fertility and the Family*, The Glover Report to the European Commission on Reproductive Technologies, London: Fourth Estate.

Hirsch, Eric (1999) Negotiated limits: interviews in south-east England, in J. Edwards, Jeanette Edwards, Sarah Franklin, Eric Hirsch, Frances Price and Marilyn Strathern (eds) *Technologies of procreation: Kinship in the age of assisted conception*, 2nd edition, London: Routledge.

Morgan, David (1989) Surrogacy: an introductory essay, in R. Lee and D. Morgan (eds) *Birthrights: Law and ethics at the beginnings of life*, London: Routledge.

Strathern, Marilyn (1998) Surrogates and substitutes: new practices for old?, in J. Good and I. Velody (eds) *The Politics of Postmodernity*, Cambridge: Cambridge University Press.

Warnock, Mary (1985) *A Question of Life: The Warnock Report on human fertilisation and embryology*, Oxford: Basil Blackwell.

Wolfram, Sybil (1989) Surrogacy in the United Kingdom, in L. M. Whiteford and M. L. Poland (eds) *New Approaches to Human Reproduction: Social and ethical dimensions*, Boulder, CO: Westview Press.

Further reading

Cook, Rachel and Shelley Day Sclater (forthcoming) *Surrogate Motherhood: International perspectives*, Cambridge: Cambridge University Press.
Ragone, Helena (1994) *Surrogate motherhood: Conception in the heart*, Boulder: Westview Press.

Biography

Marilyn Strathern gained her PhD at Cambridge University and has under-taken fieldwork in Papua New Guinea. Currently Professor of Social Anthro-pology at the University of Cambridge and Mistress of Girton College, she sits on the Nuffield Council of Bioethics. A fellow of the British Academy, and Foreign Hon. Member of the American Academy of Arts & Sciences, she was recently presidential Chair of the European Association of Social Anthro-pologists. Ethnographic investigations in gender relations (*Women in Between*, 1972) and kinship (*Kindship at the Core*, 1981) led to a critical appraisal of ongoing models of Melanesian societies (*The Gender of the Gift*, 1988), and to some extent of consumer society in Britain (*After Nature*, 1992). The debates around legislation following the Warnock Report stimulated her interest in reproductive technologies and a collaborative research project (1990–91) exam-ining some of the issues in the context of kinship was published as *Technologies of Procreation* (1993). The recently edited collection *Audit Cultures* (2000) touches on the institutionalisation of good practice.

Part IV
Genetic screening

10 Genetic testing and screening

A mixed blessing?

Jon Turney

If you were born in the UK, you have already been screened for a genetic disease. As in many other countries, a drop of blood is taken from the heel of every newborn baby, and sent off for lab tests. One of the tests – the first to be used, in around 1960 – identifies children who have more than the usual amount of a particular chemical in their blood. Those who have too much of the chemical, phenylalanine, are then looked at more closely.

That is because some of them will have the genetic disorder phenylketonuria (PKU). If they do, their cells cannot make a particular protein, an enzyme, which helps them digest phenylalanine, a component of many proteins. Accumulation of phenylalanine in the body causes mental retardation. But it can be prevented by putting children with PKU on a special diet.

This whole procedure is an example of *screening* because there is no selection of individuals for testing. It is applied, in this case, to the whole population. And most people think this is a good idea. There are drawbacks (there always are). The tests have to be applied carefully to avoid diagnosing PKU in babies who do not have it (false positives in the trade). Putting them on a phenylalanine restricted diet is harmful. For those who do have PKU, the diet is boring and costly. And a girl with PKU who grows up to have children must have a special diet during pregnancy, too.

But, on the whole, PKU testing works. The condition is pretty rare, but it used to cause about one in 100 cases of serious mental retardation. These have now been virtually eliminated. And although 15,000 babies are tested for every one found to have PKU, it still saves money.

You might think, then, that the promise of a whole lot more genetic screening – based on our new, very detailed knowledge of genes and DNA rather than on testing blood chemicals – would be good news. But if we look more closely at the PKU test, we can see why other screening programmes might not be so straightforward to assess.

In PKU a whole set of features come together to make screening successful. It is a simple condition, genetically speaking. Everyone is equally likely to be exposed to the chemical which causes the damage to affected individuals because we all eat it. The test, if properly carried out, is reliable. It is easy to interpret, in the sense that the outcome of untreated PKU is pretty much a certainty. It involves a condition present at birth, but the test is done on the baby, not the parent or the foetus. And there is a relatively simple and effective treatment. Even then, the experience of PKU testing has revealed some pitfalls as well as great benefits, as historian Diane Paul points out (Paul, 2000). Few other tests exhibit all these features, and varying any one of them makes it much harder to decide whether screening is a good idea.

To see how, let's look at the slightly more complicated case of cystic fibrosis (CF). This is caused by a gene which occurs in altered form in about one white person in twenty. They are healthy carriers, as their other copy of the gene works properly: CF is a recessive disorder. When two carriers have a child, on average one in four of the children will have two copies of an altered form of the gene, and show signs of the disease. These include sticky mucus in the lungs, which leads to infections, and problems with digestion.

In 1989 the gene involved in CF was identified, and in theory it is now easy to test prospective parents to see if an 'unhealthy' gene variant is carried by one or both of them. But the test is not completely reliable. The gene for the protein which does not do its job properly in people with CF, known as CFTR, is a large one, and nearly 1,000 different mutations have now been found in the DNA code. Although many of these are rare, even the best testing now on offer only picks up 85 per cent of couples at risk of having an affected child.

Now put yourself in the position of someone who has tested positive for one of the common alterations in the gene. You can suggest that your partner has the test, too. But if their test is negative, you cannot be *absolutely* sure there is no risk if the two of you have a child. If it is positive, the only way to be sure your child will not have CF is to have another, prenatal, test, using the unborn child's DNA. If that shows that the foetus has two copies of the affected gene, you may choose to have an abortion.

On the other hand, you may have moral objections to abortion. Or you may just be an optimist. CF causes premature death, but it does not induce a profound handicap like PKU. The treatments are not much good, but they are getting better. Life expectancy for people with CF is increasing all the time, though it is still low. There is talk of gene therapy to correct the defect, which might even become possible in your child's lifetime. All this you have to weigh up in making your decision. You may feel that the offer of the genetic test for CF has made your life more complicated, not simpler, more stressful rather than less.

These complexities arise when only a few of the features which made PKU simple to think about were changed. Cystic fibrosis is still a relatively simple condition. Only one gene is involved, and the probability that you will have the disease if you are born with two altered copies of the gene is very high (though not 100 per cent, and the severity of the symptoms varies).

Other screening tests likely to be on offer in future will differ in other ways from PKU. Two extremely important differences are that they will more often involve conditions which affect people later in life – 'late onset' disorders – and they will concern illnesses influenced by many different things – multifactorial conditions. There are many risk factors for heart disease, for instance, including fatty diets, lack of exercise and smoking. Will we regard having a few dodgy genes as just another risk factor, or will they seem specially important *because* they are genes? Similar questions arise for many forms of cancer. The third complication to note is that new technologies, like so-called 'gene chips', are likely to make it easy to screen for many genes at once.

What does this mean? The result of a single screening test will not mean that you have a problem (or are free of it), and will not mean that if you have it you have it now. It will mean that you might be susceptible, you may be more at risk, something unpleasant may happen to you, one day. Then again, it might not. Now what do you do?

For example, we know that one of several proteins involved in blood transport of the fatty chemicals called lipids, apolipoproteinE, occurs in three different versions. If you have two copies of the gene for APOE4, and 7 per cent of people in Europe do, you have a 90 per cent chance of getting Alzheimer's disease when you are older. Worse, the devastating symptoms of Alzheimer's, including loss of memory and, ultimately, identity, are likely to begin in your late sixties instead of, as in the majority of cases, in your eighties.

But why would you want to know? There is, as yet, no treatment, and no real idea how to prevent the disease. Will it help you to be told, if you know the disease has cropped up in your family, that you yourself are at high or low risk? Most doctors and ethicists doubt it will help (Post *et al.*, 1997). And who else are you going to tell, and when?

A case like this also raises other problems. Does a doctor who gets a result from such a test have any obligation to other members of the patient's family? Do insurance companies have any right to ask about such a test? If they do not, what is to stop someone who has tested positive from buying loads of extra life insurance? Would it be helpful to have granny tested before taking out a mortgage on that house with the downstairs flat attached, so you can keep an eye on her as she grows older? One writer has wondered what would have happened if someone had tested some of the already elderly Ronald Reagan's cells for the DNA signature of Alzheimer's when he was running for US president (Ridley, 1999). We certainly know that he came down with the disease soon after he left the White House.

This is not to say that susceptibility tests like this may not bring benefits. The same apolipoprotein genes, for instance, are implicated in heart disease, and people with particularly risky combinations can watch their diet. As Ridley puts it, 'the medical profession must soon learn to seek which of us could profit from such a warning and which of us can relax and hit the ice cream' (p. 261). But this perhaps suggests a clear cut difference between risk categories which may not often appear.

It also assumes a rather simple response to warnings about risk. But such responses tend to be anything but simple. Research suggests that people's reactions to being told they may face a genetic risk can range from denial – 'it won't happen to me' – to fatalism – 'I'm going to get it anyway, so there's nothing I can do'. Neither response produces the preventive response which would actually help some people.

Mention of prevention also points to another, broader concern. If medicine comes to focus on identifying people at higher risk of common conditions like heart disease or cancers, will that discourage more general preventive efforts, whether based on health education or, say, alleviating the poverty which may make it harder to maintain a healthy diet?

A particularly acute form of this dilemma can arise in the workplace. For instance, the metal beryllium is essential for making nuclear weapons, among other things, but exposure to even small quantities can lead to chronic beryllium disease, a serious or even fatal lung condition. Employers try to reduce exposure to beryllium, but cannot eliminate it completely. Recently, genetic markers have been found which indicate an unusually high sensitivity to beryllium. Should the laboratory test for these, and advise those who test positive to move to different jobs? Or will this reduce the incentive to cut beryllium exposure for everyone else, or to monitor all workers for early signs of the disease?

As this suggests, there are principles which may guide use of new tests in ways which help maximise the benefits and minimise problems. They need to go beyond simple cost–benefit analyses sometimes favoured by health planners and decision-makers. If a test is voluntary then it is usually suggested this must mean some kind of *informed consent*. This can itself be quite complicated to think through. As the British Nuffield Council on Bioethics put it, 'consent to screening differs in several respects from the consent of an individual undergoing treatment, in particular in the way that families are involved' (p. 29). Then there is the business of deciding what counts as being fully informed, and how exactly to go about informing people when they may know little of the technicalities involved.

Similarly, the principle of *confidentiality* implied by the provision of 'private information' to the beryllium workers is appealing. Again, though, there are complications, as the Nuffield Council recognised. Here, they suggested that normal medical confidentiality 'might justifiably be broken if an individual refused to disclose information which might avoid grave damage to other family members' (p. 43).

All of this suggests that, along with the undoubted benefits which more widespread use of screening for more gene variants will bring, there will be problems, too. We cannot predict in detail what they will all be. For example, some people told they have an increased genetic risk for heart disease respond by working hard to minimise other risk factors – through exercise or healthy eating. But others hear the news fatalistically, and assume there is nothing they can do (Marteau and Lerman, 2001). More speculatively, some people appear to regard the presence of a genetic influence as reducing the possible stigma attached to a mental illness, like schizophrenia. But others seem to feel that the suggestion that there could be a gene in the family which leads to this kind of outcome is offensive in itself. It can depend on the particular culture, even the particular family.

This evidence that some genetic tests may turn out to be a distinctly mixed blessing is an argument for regarding each new testing programme as an experiment, and monitoring outcomes carefully. It also means that people may find it more helpful than in the past to learn about genes and genetic technologies, because the chances that most of us will have to make sense of potentially important genetic information some time during our lives are increasing all the time (Day and Wilson, 2001).

References

Day, Ian and Wilson, David (2001) Science, medicine, and the future: genetics and cardiovascular risk, *British Medical Journal* 323: 1409–12 (15 December).

Marteau, T. and Lerman, C. (2001) Genetic risk and behavioural change, *British Medical Journal* 322: 1056–9 (28 April).

Nuffield Council on Bioethics (1993) *Genetic Screening – Ethical Issues*, London: Nuffield Council on Bioethics.

Paul, Diane (2000) A double-edged sword, *Nature* 405: 515.

Post, S. G., Whitehouse, P. J., Binstock, R. H., Bird, T. D., Eckert, S. K., Fairer, L. A., Fleck, L. M., Gaines, A. D., Juengst, E. T., Karlinsky, H., Miles, S., Murrary, T. H., Quaid, K. A., Relkin, N. R., Roses, A. D., St. George-Hyslop, P. H., Sachs, G. A., Steinbock, B., Truschke, E. F. and Zinn, A. B. (1997) The clinical introduction of genetic testing for Alzheimer's Disease: an ethical perspective, *Journal of the American Medical Association* 277(10): 832–6.

Ridley, Matt (1991) *Genome: The Autobiography of a Species in 23 Chapters*, London: Fourth Estate.

Further reading

Advisory Committee on Genetic Testing (1998) *Genetic Testing for Late Onset Disorders*, 27 pp. London.

T. Marteau and R. Croyle (1998) Psychological responses to genetic testing, *British Medical Journal*, 316: 693–6, 28 Feb.

Scope Note 22 – *Genetic Testing and Screening*, National Reference Center for Bioethics Literature. Accessible at http://bioethics.georgetown.edu.

Note: All *British Medical Journal* citations can be accessed freely at www.bmj.com

Biography

Jon Turney lectures in science communication in the Department of Science and Technology Studies at University College London. He has a particular interest in public understanding of the life sciences. He is the author of *Frankenstein's Footsteps: Science, Genetics and Popular Culture* (Yale, 1998), and editor of the Icon Books popular history series *Revolutions in Science.*

11 Genetic screening for sickle cell and thalassaemia

Can we learn anything from the UK experience?

Elizabeth N. Anionwu

Introduction

The Human Genome Project has encouraged a debate about the implications of prospective parents becoming aware of some of the genetic characteristics they could pass on to their children. The pros and cons of screening to detect, and possibly prevent, the transmission of a serious genetic illness are now regularly debated in newspaper articles, radio chat shows and television programmes.

On the one hand, it is argued that individuals could take advantage of this newly emerging technology and have the opportunity to become aware of their 'genetic status' before they have a child. Whilst this is generally considered to be the preferred time to consider the options, it is also recognised that pregnancy is often the first time that screening is routinely undertaken within the National Health Service (NHS). The main purpose, both before or during pregnancy, is for couples to decide whether they want to consider the option of preparing for, or preventing, the birth of a child with a serious disorder.

On the other hand, there are concerns about whether health professionals such as general practitioners, obstetricians and midwives are able to ensure that genetic screening is truly voluntary and backed up with adequate information and genetic counselling. Can a system such as the NHS ensure that couples are informed, confident and supported enough to decide whether or not to embark on the sometimes helter-skelter journey of genetic screening, whatever the outcome may be?

The media coverage often gives the impression that these are very new concepts without recognising that there are already examples of genetic screening programmes within the NHS. This contribution will focus on what lessons can be learnt from the last three decades of screening for sickle cell and thalassaemia, inherited conditions that primarily affect black and minority groups. There will be an exploration of the ethical and social issues surrounding the delivery of screening programmes, particularly during pregnancy. Prior to this a brief overview will be provided of the commonest of these disorders, sickle cell anaemia and beta thalassaemia major (Anionwu and Atkin, 2001).

What are sickle cell and thalassaemia disorders?

Sickle cell anaemia and beta thalassaemia major are disorders of haemoglobin, the oxygen-carrying protein inside red blood cells. The conditions are inherited in an autosomal recessive manner, which means that they are equally distributed between boys and girls and that the child with the illness has received two copies of the sickle or thalassaemia genes, one from *each* of their parents. The parents are usually healthy carriers of a trait, having received just one copy of the sickle or beta thalassaemia gene from one or other of their parents; their other parent would have passed on the usual, functioning version of the gene. Such carriers do not have an illness, so they can only find out if they have inherited one copy of the sickle cell or beta thalassaemia gene by a special blood test. When their status as a carrier is identified, they need to be reassured that they are well and that the chance of their having a child with the illness depends upon the genetic status of their partner. If the partner has two normal copies of the gene in question, the two of them cannot have a child with sickle cell anaemia or beta thalassaemia major. Instead their children would either inherit the usual two normal copies of the gene or be a healthy carrier of the trait. Should their partner also carry the same trait as they do, the two of them could have a child with the illness in question.

In the UK it is estimated that there are about 800 individuals with thalassaemia disorders and some 10,000–12,500 people who have a sickle cell disorder. This compares with an estimated 7,500 people affected by another inherited illness, cystic fibrosis (source: Cystic Fibrosis Trust website www.cftrust.org.uk).

Sickle cell and thalassaemia disorders mainly affect individuals who are descended from families where one or more members originated from parts of the world where one type of malaria, falciparum malaria, was, or still is, endemic. This includes people who have originated from many parts of Africa, the Caribbean, the Mediterranean (including southern Italy, northern Greece and southern Turkey), South East Asia, and the Middle and Far East. The reason for this is that young children who have one copy of the sickle cell or thalassaemia gene are afforded partial protection against the life-threatening complications of falciparum malaria. In contrast, children who are born with two copies of the sickle cell or thalassaemia genes are more likely to die from the effects of falciparum malaria.

The world-wide distribution of the sickle cell and thalassaemia genes is much greater now due to a) the historical movements of at-risk populations to North and South America, the Caribbean and Western Europe, and b) inter-ethnic unions. It is important to note that white people can also be carriers or have the illnesses. The number of people who are healthy carriers for sickle cell anaemia or beta thalassaemia is far higher (by a factor of approximately 20 to 25 in the UK) than the number of those born with either of the illnesses. As already discussed, there are many ethnic groups at higher risk of being a carrier of these traits so the following are just some examples. About one in four west Africans and one in ten people of African-Caribbean origin carry the sickle cell gene. Approximately one in seven Cypriots and one in twelve Pakistanis carry the beta thalassaemia gene (as do 1 in 1,000 white British).

Sickle cell anaemia

Under certain conditions the red blood cells of a person with sickle cell anaemia can 'sickle', i.e. change from a doughnut shape to something resembling a half-moon or farmer's sickle. Triggers that can induce sickling of the red blood cells include reduced fluid in the body, fever, infections, changes in temperature and over-exertion. However, some of the factors are still not known.

Consequences of sickle cell anaemia include mild to excruciating bouts of pain, anaemia, damage to various organs in the body, e.g. spleen, lungs, hips, eyes or brain (stroke), and a vulnerability to serious and life-threatening infections. It is a variable and unpredictable illness. Early diagnosis through newborn screening programmes enables the young child to be given antibiotics to prevent life-threatening infections. Other forms of management include avoidance of sickling triggers and treatment of the severe episodes of pain and any of the other possible complications. Some individuals are now being treated with a drug called hydroxyurea, which raises the level of fetal haemoglobin in an attempt to reduce the frequency of sickling within the red blood cells.

Whilst there are still some early deaths, life expectancy of an individual with sickle cell anaemia is improving, with many surviving into their forties or more. A few children have been cured through bone marrow transplants but important problems exist with this technique. These include finding a compatible donor, possible serious side effects and a 10% mortality rate. There is thus considerable debate about how parents and professionals can balance these risks against the difficulty of predicting which affected individuals will have a longer and reasonable quality of life and which may die at an early age or have a very painful and impaired life.

Beta thalassaemia major

People with beta thalassaemia major cannot produce sufficient amounts of haemoglobin to avoid a fatal anaemia unless they receive blood transfusions every 4–6 weeks of their life. A major complication of this treatment is that excess iron from the transfusions cannot be excreted from their body. It ends up being stored in the liver, heart and endocrine glands, causing life-threatening damage unless the individual also has chelation therapy which helps the excess iron to be excreted from the body. This entails the drug being injected over a 7-hour period for five to seven days a week. Not surprisingly, young adults find this regimen very difficult to undertake on a regular basis. Whilst life expectancy has improved into the thirties and forties, a significant number of early deaths occur due to non-adherence to this treatment. Heart and/or liver failure due to iron overload then results. Additional complications of beta thalassaemia major can include diabetes and osteoporosis.

Bone marrow transplants are more commonly undertaken than is the case for sickle cell anaemia, with about 25% on the UK thalassaemia register having had one. Future therapies include a greater use of hydroxyurea (see sickle cell anaemia above) and, in the longer term, the possibilities of gene therapy.

Individuals and their families affected by sickle cell anaemia and beta thalassaemia also need socio-psychological support and access to better informed professionals.

Why screen for sickle cell and thalassaemia?

A variety of reasons exist as to why screening for sickle cell and thalassaemia is, or might be, carried out, including:

- *To diagnose the disorder in newborn babies* Research findings (e.g. Gaston et al., 1986) revealed that death rates in children with sickle cell anaemia can be drastically reduced or avoided if a) the illness is identified from birth and b) affected babies are then started on a prophylactic dose of penicillin to prevent them succumbing to the effects of pneumococcal pneumonia, meningitis or septicaemia (blood poisoning).
- *To detect carriers of sickle cell or thalassaemia* During the 1960s to the mid-1980s the diagnosis of the disorder in children led to a first realisation for a significant number of parents in the UK that these conditions ran in their families. The process leading up to this may have been very tortuous with constant visits to the GP or hospital. Couples were shocked to discover that the child had inherited the illness from both of them. Anger was also experienced in those cases where they discovered that a previous blood test had already identified that one or other of them was known to carry the gene in question. Either they had not been informed by their general practitioner (or other health professional) or they had not been offered genetic counselling to explain the result. Referring to lack of information from GPs, one specialist worker explained: 'It is just that the information the GPs give sometimes is a bit "Oh, go away, it is alright, there is nothing to worry about" and people want more than that . . . I have had instances where I have sent a letter off to somebody, saying I am going to come and see you to discuss the results, and they have said "Oh there is no need to come, doctor said . . . there was nothing to worry about" (Atkin et al., 1998, p. 1642).

  Alternatively, the parents realised that they had never been tested and wondered why, if it was such a straightforward investigation, it had not been done when they had had a previous blood test or during pregnancy.

  Some individuals may not wish, for many reasons, to find out that they are carriers. The process of arriving at this knowledge may be too daunting, including the thought of a blood test because of a fear of needles. The decisions that suddenly face you once you do find out you are a carrier are not straightforward. For example, would you tell the person you would like to be your partner and at what stage in the relationship? Would you split up if s/he was also found to be a carrier or are there other issues concerning a relationship that you consider to be equally, if not more, important than your genetic screening results? If you decided to stay together, how would you feel about having children at risk of a sickle cell or beta thalassaemia disorder? Would you decide to take a chance and see what happens, not have any children at all, adopt or have fewer children than planned? Or would you undergo prenatal diagnosis, as described next?

- *To provide an option for testing the unborn baby* Genetic testing of the unborn baby (prenatal diagnosis) for sickle cell anaemia was first carried out in the late 1970s (Kan and Dozy, 1978). There are various techniques that can be undertaken as early as the eleventh week of pregnancy – all have risks of miscarriage associated with them.

  If the illness is diagnosed in the unborn baby, the couple can then decide whether to continue with the pregnancy or to request that it be terminated. They need to be offered information and counselling throughout the whole of this difficult period to enable them to make whatever decision is appropriate for them.

  Pre-implantation genetic diagnosis is a technique for identifying those embryos at the eight cell stage that have the genes for a genetic condition. A drug that stimulates ovulation is administered to the mother-to-be, the eggs are removed from the womb and fertilised externally. A cell is removed from the embryos and is tested for genes resulting in the condition, using a 'gene chip'. Healthy embryos may be implanted in the womb and affected embryos are discarded. This technique is now legally used in the UK for sickle cell and thalassaemia, with or without the use of fertility treatment. There has been considerable coverage in the media (for example, see the *Guardian*, 2 October 2001, page 11; *BBC Online News*, 13 December 2001 (www.news.bbc.co.uk); and the *Mail on Sunday*, 16 December 2001, page 33) of a couple who wish to use the technique to try not only to have an unaffected child but one that would also be a compatible bone marrow donor for their son, who has beta thalassaemia major. The couple want their son to undergo a bone marrow transplant, which if successful would be the only possibility of a cure for the condition. The technique requires finding a compatible donor, ideally a brother or sister. The couple have four other unaffected children, but none of them is a compatible match.

What screening is carried out at present?

A recent examination of the history of service provision for sickle cell and thalassaemia highlighted the experience of parents, affected individuals and at-risk communities (Anionwu and Atkin, 2001). The detailed evaluation reviewed the literature over the last two decades, including that emanating from research and publications from user groups (e.g. Sickle Cell Society, 1981) and academics (e.g. Atkin *et al.*, 1998). Whilst noting that there have been some improvements during this period, the review still identified current problems in respect of genetic screening for these conditions, including:

- ad-hoc, poorly co-ordinated and inadequately resourced services leading to inequitable information, screening and genetic counselling provision;
- a marginalised service not linked to regional clinical genetic centres;
- inadequate language support;
- low status afforded to the issue by general practitioners;
- delays in screening, particularly during pregnancy;
- perception of subtle and overt pressures to terminate affected unborn babies;
- concerns held by some professionals about the lower uptake of prenatal diagnosis and termination of pregnancies in respect of sickle cell anaemia compared to beta thalassaemia major;
- inappropriate generalisations about the attitudes of black and minority groups towards screening;
- poorly informed health professionals;
- institutional and individual racism;
- a few areas in the country where practice was culturally and linguistically sensitive and valued by users. This was particularly the case in those districts that employed specialist sickle cell and thalassaemia counsellors, usually black and minority ethnic midwives and nurses (see Atkin *et al.*, 1998);
- decisions about who should be screened based on inaccurate perceptions of ethnicity: 'Carriers were often not identified and the condition sometimes mis-diagnosed, if the person did not fit these ethnic stereotypes of "at-risk" groups. Mrs Morris (name has been changed), for example, did not look Asian or African-Caribbean and was thus not regarded as being "at risk", despite concerns about her daughter. *They kept telling me, all superior like, "Oh no, you are the wrong ethnic background"*. Her daughter was eventually diagnosed as having SCD' (Atkin *et al.*, 1998, p. 1641).

Problems to be addressed

A major problem concerns the poorly debated tensions surrounding the current conflicting objectives of screening programmes, i.e. *informed decision-making* and *prevention*. How well do health professionals support couples to make an informed decision? Are midwives, general practitioners and obstetricians providing enough information in a way that it is understood? How well do they respect the impact on the couple of religion, personal philosophy, health beliefs, culture and views on disability and the termination of pregnancy? Do the professionals knowingly or unknowingly exert undue pressure on the woman with regard to whether or not to undergo screening procedures? Are all the possible implications of different results explained in a way that is understood by people who cannot read very well or where English is not the first language? What follow-up support is provided to couples regardless of the decision they ultimately make? There also appears to be a dearth of specialist training programmes that can assist relevant health professionals to become competent and confident in exploring all these issues.

Conclusion

Fortunately, there have been some very positive developments. The NHS Plan that was announced in July 2000 included a resourced commitment that by 2004 there will be a national linked antenatal and neonatal screening programme for sickle cell and thalassaemia (for more details see www-phm. umds.ac.uk/haemscreening/). This will be undertaken in full collaboration with key user groups and embrace an information component for both the public and professionals. There is no doubt that pressure exerted by interested professionals, user groups and some political organisations led to this timely development. Unfortunately, the labelling of these conditions as 'minority ethnic' genetic disorders is still having an impact on decisions about who should or should not be screened. It is of interest that the proposal to screen *all* newborn babies for cystic fibrosis is seen as efficient because there is no need to separate out 'non-white' babies. In contrast, there has been much agonising about the expense that would be incurred if all, including 'white' babies, were screened for sickle cell anaemia.

The antenatal screening programme will be closely linked with enhancements underway to ensure a better information and support infrastructure for women and their partners during screening programmes for conditions such as Down's syndrome. This is being led by the National Screening Committee (see www.nsc.nhs.uk). What is still needed is a similar resourced countrywide strategy to improve the quality of care for those who have the illness. Otherwise fears of eugenic overtones will be raised, if it appears that the emphasis of NHS funding is solely on a national programme for genetic screening. Future genetic screening programmes can certainly learn from the problems of a sickle and thalassaemia screening programme that historically was not given a high enough status at a national level. It is ironic that sickle cell anaemia was the first condition to be recognised as a 'molecular disorder' in 1949 by Linus Pauling and colleagues. It is to be hoped that it does not take this long for new genetic screening advances to be applied in a manner that, from the outset, takes on board the implications for individuals from ethical, social, ethnic, scientific and policy perspectives.

References

Anionwu, E.N. and Atkin, K. (2001) *The Politics of Sickle Cell and Thalassaemia* (Buckingham: Open University Press).

Atkin, K., Ahmad, W.I.U and Anionwu, E.N. (1998) Screening and counselling for sickle cell disorders and thalassaemia: the experience of parents and health professionals, *Social Science and Medicine,* 47(11): 1639–51.

Gaston, M.H., Verter, J.I., Woods, G., Kelleher, J., Presbury, G., Zarkowsky, H., Vichinsky, E., Iyer, R., Lobel, J.S., Diamond, S., Holbrook, C.T., Gill, F.M., Ritchey, K. and Falletta, J.M. (1986) Prophylaxis with oral penicillin in children with sickle cell anaemia: a randomized trial, *New England Journal of Medicine,* 314: 1593–9.

Kan, Y.W. and Dozy, A.M. (1978) Antenatal diagnosis of sickle cell anemia by DNA analysis of amniotic fluid cell, *Lancet,* 11: 910–12.

Pauling, L., Itano, H.A., Singer, S.J. and Wells, I.C. (1949) Sickle cell anaemia, a molecular disease, *Science,* 110: 543–8.

Sickle Cell Society (1981) *Sickle Cell Disease: The Need for Improved Services* (London: Sickle Cell Society).

Further reading and resources

Anionwu, E.N. and Atkin, K. (2001) *The Politics of Sickle Cell and Thalassaemia.* (Buckingham: Open University Press).

Further details about sickle cell and thalassaemia can be obtained from the websites of the Sickle Cell Society (www.sicklecellsociety.org) and the UK Thalassaemia Society (www.ukts.org). Another useful resource is the Wired for Health website (the Health Development Agency oversees its development) www.wiredforhealth.gov.uk. Information about sickle cell and thalassaemia are contained in the Mind, Body and Soul section, which aims to give young people aged 14–16 the lowdown on health which has an element of fun and in an interesting way. It also contains material to help them with their schoolwork, for example in Key Stages 3 and 4 of the National Curriculum.

The NHS Haemoglobinopathy Screening Programme website www-phm.umds. ac.uk/haemscreening/ provides details concerning the implementation of this programme by the year 2004 as set out in the NHS Plan.

The Human Genetics Commission (HGC) website www.hgc.gov.uk is another useful site. The HGC analyses current and potential developments in human genetics and advises ministers on the likely impact on human health and healthcare. This includes their social, ethical, legal and economic implications. The website of the National Screening Committee (NHS) www.nsc.nhs.uk includes information sheets plus details about the activities of the Antenatal and Child Health Screening subgroups. Policy positions on various conditions can be found on www.nelh.nhs.uk/screening/

Biography

Elizabeth N. Anionwu is Professor of Nursing and head of the Mary Seacole Centre for Nursing Practice at Thames Valley University. Previously, she was head of the Brent Sickle and Thalassaemia Counselling Centre, the first to be established in Britain, and then organised over twenty 'Genetic Counselling for the Community' courses based at the Unit of Clinical Genetics and Fetal Medicine at the Institute of Child Health in London. Elizabeth is a member of the Human Genetics Commission and the Antenatal Screening subgroup of the National Screening Committee.

Part V
Genetic engineering of people

12 Curing what? Curing when? Curing how?

Gene therapy and disabled people

Bill Albert

'Two elderly women are at a Catshill Mountain Resort and one of 'em says "Boy, the food at this place is really terrible". The other one says "Yeah I know, and such small portions".'

(Woody Allen, from the film *Annie Hall*, 1977)

For most people reproductive genetics poses the most difficult ethical questions – essentially what lives are worth living and what choices prospective parents should be allowed to make. For many disabled people, especially those of us with a genetic impairment, these questions take on a more personal and sinister meaning. If society condones searching out and eliminating people like me, what does this say about how I am valued by others and how I should value myself?

While these societal ethical debates (as opposed to the more narrowly defined discussions of medical ethics) continue around reproductive genetics, much less attention has been given to either the impact on disabled people of the gene therapy project or the social meaning of gene therapy for disabled people.

At first glance it might seem that similar problems do not arise with respect to genetic-based therapies, whose target is the impairment not the potential person. Surely gene therapy is simply a medical intervention, akin, for example, to inoculation. Do people who have had polio object to the development of the Salk vaccine? Have these people been devalued by the virtual eradication of the disease? What, in short, should concern disabled people about gene therapy?

'Such small portions'

We could start with the most obvious fact, one which concerns everyone. Despite the billions of dollars spent and a decade of orchestrated hype from the biotech-medical industry, there has been no gene therapy which has worked consistently. Furthermore, for those disabled people and their families who were persuaded that such treatment offered a real hope for cure, there must be disappointment that the focus has shifted away so sharply from the initial concentration on hereditary single-gene impairments. By 1996 in the US only 10% of gene therapy trials were for inherited genetic conditions, while over 70% were concerned with cancer (Martin, 1999, p. 24). The same trend is apparent in the UK.

According to the UK's Gene Therapy Advisory Committee (GTAC) this rapid change of emphasis came about principally because:

> While gene therapy for cancers have a clear commercial value, financial returns on single gene disorders may be perceived as potentially low. . . . In addition, whilst treatments for cancers had potentially multiple thera-peutic targets, single gene disorders were more likely to yield to one form of gene therapy that will work for that particular disorder based on its biology. This has rendered single gene disorders less attractive targets for funding from industry.
>
> (GTAC, 2001)

This is part of the explanation for there having been 'such small portions'.

Writing about treatments for cystic fibrosis, Alan Stockdale has observed that, contrary to popular belief, gene therapy is not really about correcting a faulty gene. Instead, if successful these therapies 'are likely to have limited and variable effects, might have to be readministered at regular intervals and used in combi-nation with other therapies. . . . Although rarely discussed, gene therapy is also likely to be expensive, particularly for diseases like CF that have relatively small populations, a not insignificant issue given the ongoing crisis in access to afford-able healthcare' (Stockdale, 1999, p. 81). As cystic fibrosis is one of the most common genetic impairments, this issue is clearly going to be of even more significance for the many other and much rarer genetic conditions.

Another, perhaps more fundamental, reason for the inability to deliver on promises was given by the man who in 1991 pioneered the first gene therapy protocols in the United States, William French Anderson. Speaking at a 1998 symposium entitled 'Engineering the Human Germline' at the University of California, Los Angeles (UCLA), he put the case for the failure of gene therapy as follows:

> The unfortunate fact is that, with the exception of a few anecdotal cases, there is no evidence of a gene therapy protocol that helps in any disease situation. Our bodies have spent tens of thousands of years learning how to protect themselves from having exogenous DNA get into their genomes. So we were all a little naive to think that if we made a viral vector and put it into the human body it would work. The body's done a very good job of recognising viral sequences and inactivating them. So the answer to your straightforward question 'Does gene therapy work?' is, at this point in time, it does not work.
>
> (UCLA, 1998)

It is because of the apparent failure of somatic gene therapy (targeting an individual) to deliver that he and many of his colleagues want to begin developing germ-line therapy (targeting an individual and their progeny). However, because of serious ethical and practical concerns, this form of gene therapy, better described as human genetic engineering, is still prohibited in most countries.

Yet another explanation for the failure of gene therapy is offered by Richard Lewontin, who, writing more generally about the promise of the Human Genome Project, says:

> The prevention or cure of metabolic and developmental disorders depends on a detailed knowledge of the mechanisms operating in cells and tissues above the level of genes, and there is no relevant information about those mechanisms in DNA sequences. In fact, if I know the DNA sequence of a gene I have no hint about the function of a protein specified by that gene, or how it enters into an organism's biology.
>
> (Lewontin, 1997)

There have been two recent (2000) cases of apparent gene therapy successes, one in France for treating babies with severe combined immunodeficiency (SCID) and the other in the US with hemophilia patients. These have prompted Larry Thompson, editor of the US Food and Drug Administration's *Consumer Magazine*, to write: 'It's true that dramatic cures have not been seen to date, but there are tantalizing signs that important advances may be just around the corner' (Thompson, 2000). While this may be true, it is an all too familiar refrain. Similar claims have been made almost weekly for the last decade.

With no effective somatic gene therapy and even people like French Anderson admitting that we are probably decades away from successful germ-line therapy, where does this leave people with genetic impairments right now and, indeed, for many years to come? Of course, we can talk about 'what if' forever. Fantasy has its place, but let's instead talk about what is. And 'what is' is simple. Research which underpins gene therapy is continuing to identify more targets for prenatal testing and the only proven way to prevent the vast majority of genetic conditions is abortion following a genetic test or embryo selection as part of IVF. It is likely that this is all that will be available for quite some time, especially if we factor in the comparative costs of cure as opposed to testing and termination.

'The food is terrible'

All that the gene therapy project seems to offer is promises. Not only are the promises premature and probably unrealistic but they have continually raised and then dashed the hopes of disabled people and their families. Many of us have been there. Many of us still are. Being tested and probed, asked to serve as living subjects for medical students and researchers – objects for the medical experts, having to fight to be the subjects of our own lives.

The gene therapy research into cystic fibrosis in the United States is a case in point. Alan Stockdale has argued that people with CF have been used essentially as research fodder. 'The process has reduced the desires and the needs of people with CF to a cure at all costs. This suggests a lack of understanding of the way in which people live with and experience the disease. The CFF's [Cystic Fibrosis Foundation] choice to focus on research for a 'cure' has meant that the many other potentially competing needs of people with CF and their families, such as CF education, social support, and age-appropriate care, have been marginalized' (Stockdale, 1999, p. 93).

This is the crux of the problem. A concentration on gene therapy cannot but construct people with genetic impairments as those impairments, so legitimising the medical model of disability and all the negative effects which follow in its wake. The paradox is that attempts to devise therapies which researchers claim may lead to people enjoying a better quality of life in the long term can have entirely the opposite effect in the short and medium term. There are no simple answers to this dilemma, especially because of the way in which the research into gene therapy is carried out, financed and marketed.

Much so-called gene therapy 'research' should be more accurately defined as experiments on human subjects. It can be extremely arduous, if not painful. One experiment on a young man with Duchenne's muscular dystrophy involved giving 188 injections under general anaesthesia (Lyon and Gorner, 1996, p. 380). This was but phase one of the experiment. In 1999, a 'gene therapy experiment at the University of Pennsylvania led to the death of Jesse Gelsinger, an 18-year-old man with an inherited metabolic disease' (Hopkins Tanne, 2000; also reported in Thompson, 2000). Subsequent revelations revealed that there had been other unexplained deaths during US gene-therapy trials and this as well as almost 700 cases of 'serious adverse events' (Nelson and Weiss, 2000) demonstrates that gene therapy is also a very risky business. Besides the immense complexity of the procedures, a good part of that risk arises precisely because it is a 'business'. Corporate involvement in the development of gene therapy and the fact that many researchers have financial ties to these companies raises clear conflict of interest questions. This all becomes more worrying because gene therapy is sold as 'hope' for people often desperate for a cure and it is these people who are actively encouraged to act as guinea pigs.

Public hearings after the Gelsinger case also expressed concern about the ways in which volunteers were recruited, 'using internet sites and newsletters which detailed the promise of the therapy if it worked and which stressed the need for human subjects. This type of information, placed where it would be seen by a population sensitive to the problems of living with a genetic disease, raises further issues about getting truly informed and voluntary subjects for human experimentation' (Kolehmainen, 2000).

A further highly damaging aspect of the gene therapy industry's practice is that its chimerical promises have come in a wrapping which is itself fundamentally disabling. To justify the project and keep the money coming in, disabled people have been necessarily wrapped and presented at worst as costly mistakes that could be avoided, at best as objects of pity and always, always in desperate need of charity.

I think back to my childhood in the US. The annual MD (muscular dystrophy) Telethon. A spindly boy in a wheelchair half smiling. A manic Jerry Lewis oozing sincerity all over the stage. 'Please give us money so this doesn't happen anymore.' 'This' was a person who needed to be valued, not abused by pity. And what has been the pay off for this annual ritual humiliation? Well, forty years on, fifteen years after the gene responsible for Duchenne MD was found, and we are still no nearer a cure. Maybe another fifteen years, maybe another forty years. Maybe. Maybe. And all the time families' hopes have been falsely raised and their young boys keep dying in their teens.

Commenting on this point, a man with CF said:

> At times I get the feeling from the Foundation [CF Foundation] that they want us [adults with CF] to just 'fade' away so as not to harm their pathetic fund raising campaigns. Yes pathetic. We are not all cute little children, sure to die if you [the public] don't send in donations.
>
> (Stockdale, 1999, p. 88)

Conclusion

We, people living with genetic disorders, are sons and daughters, husbands and wives, father and mothers, lovers and friends. We are not our impairments, although those impairments have influenced many of our life experiences – both good and bad. Just like everyone else in fact. What disables us are societies which by seeing us essentially as our impairments marginalise us as 'the other'. Through this process we become socially imagined (and in the worst case imagine ourselves) as lesser beings; people in need of special facilities, people in need of special assistance, people in need of charity, people in need of a cure, people in need.

And what appears to meet our supposed need for a cure? Gene therapy, of course, sailing majestically into view, captained by white-coated high priests and driven by the public perception of our pitiful state, by the market and, of course, by the concomitant hot air of hyped promises.

This is not, however it may seem, to argue that medical research should be stopped. That would be crazy. Like everyone else, disabled people require medical treatment. If somatic gene therapy can eventually provide this and help relieve pain and discomfort as well as prevent the death of children, then that would be wonderful.

But, of course, in the meantime we do have more immediate needs.

What we need is for there to be a clearer understanding of the nature of the negative attitudes and widespread discrimination which disable us and of how the conception behind, and the promotion of, gene therapy have helped to exacerbate these. What we need is a greater degree of openness and honesty about the gene therapy project. What we need is no more false promises. What we need is to be fully involved in an informed manner in shaping the entire medical research process, including how money is raised and allocated to clinical and social needs.

Unless these needs are met, we will continue to be considered as little more than sufferers, victims, passive and pitiful objects of other people's benevolent concern. We will continue to be owned by the medical establishment. We will continue to be done for until we are done for.

This we most definitely do not need.

References

Gene Therapy Advisory Committee (2001) 'Gene Therapy for Inherited Disorders Workshop', Friday 2 March 2001 (http://www.doh.gov.uk/genetics/gtac/proceedings2001.htm).

Hopkins Tanne, J. (2000) 'US faces ethical issues after gene therapy death', *BMJ*, 4 March, 320: 602.

Kolehmainen, S. (2000) 'The Dangerous Promise of Gene Therapy', *Gene Watch*, Vol. 13, No. 1, February 2000 (http://www.actionbioscience.org/biotech/kolehmainen.html#Primer).

Lewontin, R. (1997) 'Billions and Billions of Demons', *New York Review*, 9 January 1997 (http://www.nybooks.com/articles/article-preview?article_id=1297).

Lyon, J. and Gorner, P. (1996) *Altered Fates: Gene Therapy and the Retooling of Human Life* (London, Norton).

Martin, P. (1999) 'Genes as drugs: the social shaping of gene therapy and the reconstruction of genetic disease', in Conrad, P. and Gabe, J. (Eds) *Sociological Perspectives on the new Genetics* (Oxford, Blackwell).

Nelson, D. and Weiss, R. (2000) 'Earlier Gene Test Deaths Not Reported: NIH Was Unaware of "Adverse Events",' *The Washington Post*, January 31, p. A1.

Stockdale, A. (1999) 'Waiting for the cure: mapping the social relations of human gene therapy research', in Conrad, P. and Gabe, J. (Eds) *Sociological Perspectives on the new Genetics* (Oxford, Blackwell).

Thompson, L. (2000) 'Human Gene Therapy, Harsh Lessons, High Hopes', *FDA Consumer Magazine*, September–October, 2000 (http://www.fds.gov/fdac/features/2000/500_gene.html).

UCLA (1998) Engineering the Human Germline Symposium, UCLA, June 1998 (http://www.ess.ucla.edu:80/huge/report.html).

Biography

Bill Albert taught economic history at the University of East Anglia from 1968 to 1992. He has been active in the disability movement for about twenty years and currently chairs the Norfolk Coalition of Disabled People. He took the lead in drafting the British Council of Disabled People's position statement on disability and genetics as well as a similar statement from Disabled People's International Europe. He is a member of the UK government's Human Genetics Commission.

13 Should we genetically engineer humans?

Michael J. Reiss

Genetic engineering of any sort is controversial. Some people see it as tampering with matters that we should leave well alone. Others hope that genetic engineering will help provide us with more food, better medicines and other benefits. But are there circumstances in which we should genetically engineer people? This is a possibility which alarms many, especially given the various abuses of eugenics in a number of Western countries in the twentieth century.

I shall restrict myself to cases where humans are themselves being genetically engineered. This means, for instance, that I won't consider such topics as xeno-transplantation – when animals such as pigs are genetically engineered to make organs from them suitable for transplantation into humans. Nor shall I look at the issues resulting from the production of such products as genetically engineered human growth hormone or vaccines – when micro-organisms, animals or plants are genetically engineered to produce human proteins.

Principles of genetic engineering

The genes that every organism carries inside itself are codes or instructions: they carry information which is used to tell the organism what chemicals it needs to make in order to survive, grow and reproduce. Genetic engineering typically involves moving genes from one organism to another. The result of this procedure, if all goes as intended, is that the chemical normally made by the gene in the first organism is now made by the second.

Genetic engineering can take place in one of two ways – one that involves the genetic engineering of germ-line cells, the other the genetic engineering of somatic cells. Germ-line cells are the cells found, in mammals, in the ovaries of a female and the testes of a male and give rise, respectively, to eggs and to sperm. Somatic cells are all the other cells in the body.

The importance of this distinction is that any genetic changes to somatic cells cannot be passed on to future generations. Changes, on the other hand, to germ-line cells can indeed be passed on to children and to succeeding generations. For this reason, changes to germ-line cells generally have wider ethical implications than changes to somatic cells.

Somatic gene therapy for human diseases

The first successful attempt to genetically engineer humans was carried out in 1990. The attempts involved patients with a very rare disorder known as severe combined immune deficiency (SCID), in which the immune system doesn't work. As a result the person is highly susceptible to infections and usually dies in childhood.

SCID can have a number of causes but is often due to an inherited deficiency in a single enzyme – adenosine deaminase (ADA). The first person with SCID to be treated with gene therapy was a 4–year-old girl called Ashanthi De Silva. She was unable to produce ADA. In 1990 some of her white blood cells were removed, and functioning versions of the ADA gene introduced into them using a virus as a vector (Fox, 1994). At the same time, she received conventional treatment. The improvement in her condition was remarkable. Now, more than ten years on, she is living a comparatively normal life, attending a typical school and so on. At present she needs regular transfusions (every few months) of genetically engineered white blood cells as the white blood cells live less than a year.

To date, many hundreds of trials for somatic gene therapy have been approved world-wide, mostly in the USA. In addition to trials on people with SCID, somatic gene therapy is being tried for a number of other conditions, including cystic fibrosis (Stern and Alton, 1998), familial hypercholesterolaemia, Duchenne muscular dystrophy, haemophilia, beta thalassaemia and cancers. In some cases, the results have been very encouraging. However, progress has been slower than hoped and it is still too early to know of how much medical use somatic gene therapy will be.

The scope of somatic gene therapy

It is easy to hope that gene therapy will soon be a cure for all our problems. However, some human diseases caused by faulty genes can already be treated quite effectively by conventional means. For example, every baby born in most Western countries is tested for the genetic disease phenylketonuria. The reason is that, provided action is taken soon after birth, the harmful consequences of the condition can be prevented.

Phenylketonuria is a condition which, if untreated, leads to the person being severely mentally retarded. Affected individuals often have convulsions and, in the past, were frequently institutionalised. In the 1950s, though, it was realised that if children with the faulty gene that causes phenylketonuria are given a diet that has only small amounts of the amino acid phenylalanine, they grow up healthy and normal.

Phenylketonuria illustrates a most important truth about human development: both genes and the environment play essential parts. Phenylketonuria is a genetic disease in the sense that it is the result of a faulty gene but the extent to which the disease manifests itself depends on the environment: a normal diet (i.e. normal environment) and the person is severely affected, a special diet (i.e. a different environment) and the person is unaffected. To describe phenylketonuria, or any other condition, as a 'genetic disease' is, at best, a convenient shorthand.

A second reason why we should not see gene therapy as the likely solution to all medical problems also relates to the roles played by genes and the environment. Frequent announcements in the press that the gene for breast cancer, cancer of the colon, Alzheimer's disease, schizophrenia or whatever has been identified may appear to offer the hope for a cure. The reality, though, is often far from this.

For one thing, knowing what causes a condition may be a valuable step in preventing it, but it is most definitely not the same thing. I am unable to speak Russian or play the violin and I know why I can't. But knowing this is no more than the first step in helping me achieve these ends. In the same way, knowing which of the many human genes causes a disease is a very long way from treating, curing or preventing it. Initially, it simply offers the possibility of genetic screening.

Additionally, diseases such as phenylketonuria are the exception, not the rule. This condition is caused by an inborn error in a single gene. However, less than 2% of our total disease load is due to errors in single genes. Most human diseases have a strong environmental component, so that genetic defects merely predispose the person to develop the condition. In addition, the genetic component is the result of many genes so that simply restoring one may not be enough.

A further point is that we are only just beginning to appreciate the extent to which the human body, and mind, can overcome genetic handicaps. Particular genetic mutations certainly increase the risk of an individual developing certain cancers or heart disease. Similarly, there may well be genetic mutations which increase one's risk of developing schizophrenia or depression. However, this is very different from saying that there is 'a gene for breast cancer' or 'a gene for schizophrenia'. In the case of breast cancer, early indications are that while a mutation in the BRCA1 gene greatly increases a woman's chance of developing breast cancer, it is still the case that at least 15% of women with this mutation do not go on to develop breast cancer. Further, it is probable that many women with a history of breast cancer in their family do not have a mutation in this gene.

So far I have confined myself to what we may term 'real human diseases'. But what of gene 'therapy' to affect traits such as intelligence, beauty, criminality and sexual preference. Will this ever be practicable?

Although there are frequent reports in the popular press of 'a gene for homosexuality' or 'a gene for criminality', the above discussion of the complexity of human disease should caution us against such simplistic notions. True, it is the case, as shown by twin studies, cross fostering and other evidence, that much human behaviour has a genetic component to it. However, attempts to find genes for homosexuality, intelligence, beauty or criminality are, at best, the first steps to understanding the rich and complex ways in which we behave.

At worst, they are misguided attempts to stigmatise certain members of society. Part of the very essence of our being human is that we, above all the other organisms with which we share this planet, have the potential to transcend much of our biological heritage.

The ethical significance of somatic gene therapy

What new ethical issues are raised by somatic gene therapy? The short answer, when we are talking about real human diseases, is: probably none. This was the conclusion reached in the UK by the report on the ethics of somatic gene therapy produced by the Clothier Committee in 1992 (Clothier Committee, 1992). Of course, somatic gene therapy is still a very new technique, and mostly at the research rather than the clinical stage. However, there is considerable agreement about how medical research and innovative practice should be regulated in the light of ethical considerations. There is little doubt that ethical considerations have so far been applied to somatic gene therapy even more stringently than to conventional medicine.

Although the UK government waited over a year to respond, it eventually accepted the recommendations of the Clothier Committee. Other countries too have permitted somatic gene therapy. Because somatic gene therapy typically involves giving a person healthy DNA to override the effects of their own malfunctioning DNA, it has been pointed out that this is not very different from giving a person a blood transfusion or organ transplant. Of course, some individuals may choose not to have a transfusion or transplant, but very few people suggest forbidding them entirely.

It is also the case that somatic gene therapy has the potential to reduce the number of ethically problematic decisions. For example, at present the only 'solution' offered to a woman who is carrying a fetus identified as having a serious genetic disorder such as cystic fibrosis or muscular dystrophy is the possibility of an abortion. Somatic gene therapy may be able to offer a more positive way forward.

However, somatic gene therapy may, in time, raise new ethical issues. Suppose, despite what we have said about the complexities of human behaviour, it does eventually transpire that somatic gene therapy could reduce the likelihood of someone being violently aggressive. What then? The simple answer is to throw one's hands up in horror and agree that such 'treatments' should be outlawed. However, one problem with this response is that most countries already spend a lot of time and effort trying to get people who have been convicted of violent crimes to be less likely to commit these again. They may attend education programmes or receive state-funded psychotherapy, for instance, in attempts to achieve these aims.

This example highlights two related issues. The first is to do with the social construction of disease. It is easy to assume that diseases are fixed, objective realities. A different approach is to accept that a disease is, in a sense, a relationship a person has with society (Reiss and Straughan, 1996). Is being four foot tall a disease? The answer tells us more about a society than it does about an individual of this height.

Some conditions are relatively unproblematic in their definition as a disease. For instance, Lesch-Nyhan disease is characterised by severe mental retardation, uncontrolled movements and self-mutilation. No cure is at present available and the person dies, early in life, after what most people would consider an unpleasant existence. It is the existence of conditions such as this that have even led to claims in the courts of wrongful life or wrongful birth, where a sufferer, or someone acting on their behalf, sues either their parent(s) or doctor(s) on the grounds that it would have been better for them never to have been born.

However, years of campaigning by activists for people with disabilities have shown us the extent to which many diseases or disabilities are as much a reflection of the society in which the person lives as they are the product of the genes and internal environment of that person.

The second issue is to do with consent. It is one thing for a person convicted of a violent crime to give their informed consent to receive psychotherapy or some other treatment aimed at changing their behaviour – though even these treatments are, of course, open to abuse. It would be quite another for a parent to decide, on behalf of a fetus or baby, to let it receive somatic gene therapy to make it less aggressive.

In an attempt to set limits on the operation of somatic gene 'therapy', George Pazin, a member of the Orthodox Church and professor at the University of Pittsburgh School of Medicine in the USA, has argued:

> I am all in favour of repairing God's creation with the genetic tools that we have discovered, but I shudder to think of our trying to improve upon the creation.
>
> (Pazin, 1994, p. 151)

At the present time it may be difficult to be more precise than this. However, it is worth noting that several countries officially permit abortions only on health grounds yet, in practice, offer abortion on demand. By analogy, should the use of somatic gene therapy ever become widespread, it may be difficult to prevent it being used for cosmetic purposes, in much the same way that plastic surgery can be used both for life-saving and for trivial purposes.

Indeed, the history of cosmetic surgery provides a valuable model for a possible future for gene therapy. While some types of cosmetic surgery seem not only ethically unproblematic but definitely desirable, much of it makes many people uncomfortable and some of it seems downright unacceptable.

Nor should cosmetic surgery be thought only to be the province of the Western rich. In many Asian countries people save to have operations to make them appear more Western. Thousands of women in Korea undergo excruciatingly painful operations to remove muscle tissue from their legs to make themselves more slender – shades of *The Life and Loves of a She Devil* and *GATTACA* – while the first surgical operations in Japan to create a mimic of the Western eyelid were introduced by Mikamo-san in 1896 (Gilman, 1999).

Other examples of cosmetic surgery have been widely carried out to make people appear less Jewish, less likely to have suffered from syphilis, less Irish or more Aryan. This is not to mention the many millions of operations currently undertaken in an increasing number of countries to make people seem younger, slimmer or sexually more desirable. A significant proportion of these operations go wrong and it would be good to see some quality data on their long-term effectiveness.

Even if they do prove 'effective', their widespread adoption raises ethical questions. For example, much orthodontic work, which I would classify as cosmetic, causes considerable discomfort to children below the age at which I suspect they are able fully to give informed consent and, arguably, leads to no overall increase in happiness in the world, since any one person's greater happiness at having more regular than average teeth may be counteracted by the increased unhappiness of those with more irregular than average teeth.

Theological analyses

Theologians and others who take religious teachings seriously have not been slow to voice their opinions about genetic engineering. The most frequent response by religious writers, whether considering somatic gene therapy or germ-line therapy, is one of caution or hesitancy. Some people are concerned that we are building a tower of Babel with its top in the heavens and so moving into areas more appropriate for a creator than for created ones.

Others hesitate about the movement of genes between humans and other species, fearing that this somehow diminishes the distinctiveness of being human. For example, the notion that humans are made *imago Dei*, in the image of God, may cause some with a Christian faith to feel uncomfortable about a technology that apparently threatens to blur the dividing line between humans and the rest of the created order (cf. 1 Corinthians 15.39: 'For not all flesh is alike, but there is one kind for men, another for animals, another for birds, and another for fish'). Mary Douglas once wrote that 'holiness means keeping distinct the categories of creation' (Douglas, 1966/1984, p. 54).

On the other hand, there are religious writers who are quite positive about some sorts of genetic engineering. Ronald Cole-Turner has explored the implications of humans acting as participants, through genetic engineering, in redemption (Cole-Turner, 1993). The idea is that genetic engineering can help to overcome genetic defects caused by harmful mutations. In this way, genetic engineering can help to restore creation to a fuller, richer existence and can, Cole-Turner maintains, play an important role without encroaching on the scope of divine activity.

The ethical significance of germ-line therapy

The idea of genetic alterations to the human germ line (so that succeeding generations are affected, rather than just the individual concerned) has been rejected by a number of religious writers and organisations, as it has by many secular writers and organisations. The main arguments against human germ-line therapy are that it is too risky, that it is unnecessary or that it is wrong.

However, others, including a number of distinguished moral philosophers and some theologians, have argued that the time may come when germ-line therapy is permissible, even highly desirable. Some people believe that time is fast approaching.

At the moment it is generally acknowledged that human germ-line therapy is too risky. Researchers cannot, at present, control precisely where new genes are inserted. This raises the not insignificant danger that the inserted gene might damage an existing gene, which could lead to diseases and other problems, including cancers.

Even if this problem gets solved, germ therapy may produce some surprising consequences. For example, there is some evidence that mice that are genetically quicker learners than other mice may be more sensitive to pain. To evolutionary biologists such trade-offs make sense. There are few free lunches in life. 'Improving' an organism in one direction may have unfavourable consequences in others.

However, although human germ-line therapy may currently be too risky, it is difficult to imagine that this will continue to be the case indefinitely. It seems likely that scientists will develop methods of targeting the insertion of new genes with sufficient precision to avoid the problems that presently attend such procedures.

Further, although germ-line therapy is typically assumed to be irreversible, it is more likely, if we ever get to the point where its use is routine, that it will normally be reversible. There is no reason to suppose that if something went wrong with the results of germ-line therapy, this wrong would necessarily be visited on a person's descendants in perpetuity. The same techniques that would permit targeted germ-line therapy should permit its reversal.

Is germ-line therapy unnecessary? It is no easy matter to demonstrate that something is 'necessary'. Value judgements are involved, so that there may be genuine controversy about whether something is needed. Is the motor car necessary? Are elephants necessary? Or books on bioethics?

It is likely that most improvements that might result from germ-line therapy could also be effected by somatic gene therapy or conventional medicine. Diabetes is a case in point. However, it may prove to be the case that germ-line therapy allows such conditions to be treated better. It is possible that germ-line therapy might be able to produce certain benefits that could not be realised by any other technique. No doubt the human race would be able to get on without germ-line therapy, and one may question whether it would do much to increase the sum of human happiness. Nevertheless, at some point it may convincingly be argued that germ-line therapy is necessary for some individuals.

Making the assumption, then, that one day germ-line therapy will be both relatively safe and deemed necessary, in the sense that it can bring benefits that other approaches cannot, is it right or is it wrong? Some people have expressed the fear that germ-line therapy might be used by dictators to produce only certain types of people. This objection may assume too much of genetic engineering. Dictators have far more effective ways of controlling people.

A more likely problem is that germ-line therapy will be permitted before people have grown sufficiently accustomed to the idea. The pace of techno-logical change is so fast nowadays that some people end up feeling bewildered by new possibilities. It is worth recalling that people in many countries have grown comfortable with such practices as organ transplants and *in vitro* fertil-isation, although such procedures gave rise in the aftermath of their initial development to very considerable ethical debate (not all of which, of course, has died away – in Japan transplants remain unacceptable, as *in vitro* fertilisation is to many Roman Catholics). Similarly, perhaps human germ-line therapy will become broadly acceptable.

A frequently expressed worry about germ-line therapy is the extent to which future generations will be affected. Again, it is possible that this fear may be an exaggerated one. As we have said, we can overestimate the importance of our genetic make-up. Then there is the point that people already have and will con-tinue to have a tremendous influence over future generations through every-thing from childrearing patterns and family planning to books and pollution.

There remains the worry, though, born of long experience with slippery slopes, that the road to hell is paved with good intentions. Despite the difficul-ties of distinguishing in all cases between genetic engineering to correct faults (such as cystic fibrosis, haemophilia or cancers) and genetic engineering to enhance traits (such as intelligence, creativity, athletic prowess or musical ability), the best way forward may be to ban germ-line therapy intended only to enhance traits even if it proves to be safe, at least until many years of informed debate have taken place.

The idea that it is useful to distinguish between genetic engineering to treat disease and genetic engineering to enhance traits appeals to some theologians who have argued that genetic engineering to treat disease may be seen as part of the redemptive activity of humans. At the same time, it is worth noting the words of J. Robert Nelson, senior research fellow of the Institute of Religion, Texas Medical Centre, and adjunct professor of medical ethics at Baylor College of Medicine:

> The prospect of overcoming and even eliminating from the germ-line certain types of human suffering is, like all other eschatologies, both appealing and frightening.

> (Nelson, 1994, p. 164)

Nor is it only religious leaders who have warned of the dangers of presuming to improve human nature or enhance human capabilities. Jonathan Glover quotes the philosopher John Mackie, who once argued, against Glover's optimism about germ-line therapy, that 'if the Victorians had been able to use genetic engineering, they would have aimed to make us more pious and patriotic' (Mackie, 1984, p. 149).

Finally, it might be the case that genetic engineering would require parents to choose which traits they would like enhanced in their children. It may, for example, prove impossible simultaneously to enhance a child's ability to learn mathematics, paint, show great empathy and play a musical instrument. It can be argued that genetic engineering to enhance human traits might diminish the autonomy of the genetically engineered child that results.

Nevertheless, suppose that one day it really does become possible safely to improve everyone's IQ by some 20 to 40 points through germ-line modification. Imagine further that this procedure especially benefits those who would otherwise have an IQ of below 100 (in other words, it decreases the variance in IQ scores rather than increasing it) and that the procedure can be carried out much more effectively and cheaply than via other routes (e.g. somatic gene modification, psychosurgery or extra education). It could be that it would prove difficult to argue that such a procedure should be made illegal. Indeed, I suspect that it is more likely that we would be discussing whether it should (like education in general) be mandatory or (like school education, as opposed to education at home) optional.

References

Clothier Committee (1992) *Report of the Committee on the Ethics of Gene Therapy* (London, HMSO).

Cole-Turner, R. (1993) *The New Genesis: theology and the genetic revolution* (Louisville, Kentucky, Westminster/John Knox Press).

Douglas, M. (1966/1984) *Purity and Danger: an analysis of the concepts of pollution and taboo* (London, Routledge).

Fox, J. L. (1994) Gene therapy off to slow start, *Bio/Technology*, 12, p. 1066.

Gilman, S. L. (1999) *Making the Body Beautiful: a cultural history of aesthetic surgery* (Princeton, Princeton University Press).

Mackie, J. cited in Glover, J. (1984) *What Sort of People Should There Be?* (Harmondsworth, Middlesex, Penguin Books).

Nelson, J. R. (1994) *On the New Frontiers of Genetics and Religion* (Grand Rapids, Michigan, William B. Eerdmans Publishing Company).

Pazin, G. cited in Nelson, J. R. (1994) *On the New Frontiers of Genetics and Religion* (Grand Rapids, Michigan, William B. Eerdmans Publishing Company).

Reiss, M. J. and Straughan, R. (1996) *Improving Nature? The science and ethics of genetic engineering* (Cambridge, Cambridge University Press).

Stern, M. and Alton, E. (1998) Gene therapy for cystic fibrosis, *Biologist*, 45, pp. 37–40.

Further reading

Kitcher, P. (1996) *The Lives to Come: the genetic revolution and human possibilities* (London, Allen Lane).
Lewontin, R. C. (1993) *The Doctrine of DNA: biology as ideology* (London, Penguin).
Reiss, M. J. and Straughan, R. (1996) *Improving Nature? The science and ethics of genetic engineering* (Cambridge, Cambridge University Press).

Biography

Michael J. Reiss is Professor of Science Education at the Institute of Education, University of London, and a priest in the Church of England. He researches and lectures widely in bioethics and science education. He has been chair of EuropaBio's Advisory Group on Ethics and a specialist adviser to the House of Lords on the use of animals. He has provided advice and consultancy for a number of biotechnology and pharmaceutical companies and is a member of the ethics committee of a major infertility clinic.

Part VI
Farm animal well-being

14 Breeding and biotechnology in farm animals

Ethical issues

Christian Gamborg and Peter Sandøe

Introduction

Over the last century, and especially since the Second World War, animal production has become ever more efficient. Broiler chickens can grow to a weight of 2 kg in about five weeks, whereas forty years ago it took twelve weeks to reach the same weight, and over the same period milk yields in most dairy cows have more than doubled. These achievements derive in part from improved management techniques, but to a large and still increasing extent they are the outcome of farm animal breeding, i.e. genetic improvement.

Recently, traditional selective breeding – using the best specimens of each generation as parents for the next generation – has been increasingly supplemented by various forms of biotechnology. Thus today's breeders employ techniques such as artificial insemination and embryo transplantation to control animal reproduction. In a not very distant future it seems likely that gene technology will be exploited commercially in a routine manner as well.

The tremendous growth in productivity has added to human wealth. It has also allowed farmers to make good use of the natural resources at their disposal. However, farm animal breeding has also had a negative impact – on animal health and welfare, and on genetic diversity. And these drawbacks mean that we need to ask whether some ways of using the tools delivered by animal genetics are morally unacceptable. In particular, we ought to ask: is economically motivated animal breeding that concentrates on improved productivity and carries costs in terms of genetic diversity and animal health and welfare defensible? What limits to acceptable practice should we set in this area? And what other issues in breeding need to be looked at in the future? Greater control in this area is accompanied by a heavier burden of ethical responsibility.

These ethical questions must be faced by breeders, farmers and ultimately the rest of us. To answer them we need to understand both the science and the current practice of animal breeding. This understanding will ensure that the worries on which we focus are factually grounded and not based on erroneous assertions. But this is not enough. We also need to reflect on the values that lie behind attitudes to animal breeding – those, that is, that drive the search for improved productivity, and those that cause people to have misgivings about that search. For we need to resolve the ethical conflicts to which these values often give rise, and these conflicts will never be resolved while the parties to them lack mutual understanding of one another's perspectives and values.

Animal breeding and biotechnology

In prehistoric times wild beasts were tamed, and through generations of selection domesticated animals evolved. The domestication of animals has played a very important role in the development of our culture.

Ideally, animal breeding allows us to design future generations of domestic animals. This can, for example, be done with particular regard for production, reproduction, health and functional traits. Breeding goals vary with species, local conditions and time. Thus ancient peoples were primarily concerned to obtain meat and skin, and to develop working animals, from cattle. The cows they kept produced little milk. Today in Western Europe, by contrast, specialised cattle are bred to produce either milk or beef. In many parts of Asia and Africa oxen are still bred for characteristics that improve their quality as transport animals. Pigs, which are always bred for meat, are subjected to breeding techniques that produce high-quality pork or bacon at the lowest possible cost. Poultry have also followed this pattern of specialisation, and many breeds are now designed either to produce eggs (laying hens) or to produce meat (broilers). In laying hens, genetic selection has been for traits ensuring that more eggs are produced. In broilers, the main breeding goal has been to increase juvenile growth rates and to encourage the efficient conversion of feed to meat.

Breeding techniques have developed dramatically over the last century. Systematic recording of the productivity of dairy cows started in the late nineteenth century. Other species, such as pigs and sheep, had to wait until the early twentieth century. It was at the beginning of the twentieth century, when Mendelian genetics was rediscovered, that breeding began to evolve towards more advanced breeding practices. Since then several changes have occurred that are worth noting. These changes can be summarised as a growing focus on production combined with advanced biometrical models and the deployment of genetic technologies.

In biotechnology a distinction can be made between reproductive technology and gene technology. The former aims to control (and often accelerate) the process of breeding. The first technology of this kind to be developed was artificial insemination, which allowed reproduction to take place without natural mating. In the 1950s a technique for freezing semen enhanced the potential of artificial insemination. Semen storage made it possible to pass on valuable traits from male breeding animals to a greater number of individuals, and to transfer genes over time and across local and global geographic boundaries. Contemporary breeders are, therefore, no longer restricted by the locally available gene pool. World-wide 110 million artificial inseminations are carried out in cattle each year (Thibier and Wagner, 2002).

Similarly, technologies have been developed to enable female animals to produce many more progeny than they would naturally. These include super-ovulation, which allows several embryos/eggs to be produced per selected donor, and embryo transfer, which enables the breeder to shuttle embryos to recipients that act as surrogate mothers. A technique has also been developed that makes it possible to remove immature eggs from female animals, mature and fertilise these *in vitro,* and then transfer the fertilised eggs to recipients which serve as surrogate mothers. These technologies have been of particular value to cattle breeders, because in cattle there are long generation intervals and each cow normally produces only one calf per year.

Let us turn now to the other type of biotechnology used in animal breeding: gene technology. Gene technology makes it possible to 'map' genes. That is, it identifies the precise location of genes on chromosomes. Such mapping – which either uses direct selection of major genes or makes use of so-called genetic markers, i.e. a segment of DNA with an identifiable physical location on a chromosome whose inheritance can be followed – promises to be a very valuable aid in selective breeding. For it will allow selections to be made on the basis of genes rather than on the basis of properties of the animals to which the genes give rise.

Largely as a result of widely reported disputes over GM crops, the use of gene technology with the highest public profile is genetic engineering, i.e. in animals the direct manipulation of an organism's genetic make-up to create genetically modified animals. Here genes from the same or another species can be intro-duced into a fertilised egg so that the organism that subsequently develops inherits genes of mixed origin. The mature organism might, for example, be an animal with disease-resistance genes originating in another species. It is worth emphasising at once that, until now, animals have been genetically engineered mainly for the purpose of biomedical research. At present there are no commercially available genetically engineered farm animals. And fish breeding is the only area in which genetically modified animals appear to be in the pipeline.

As we mentioned in the introduction to this chapter, the main objective of farm animal breeding was until recently to improve production and efficiency. Among other things, the pursuit of this objective has enabled farmers to become more cost effective and maintain an income in spite of the falling prices of farm products. Quite often farmers have not really had any choice here. They have had to rely on modern breeding if they are to survive economically. However, at the same time the technological developments we have described have caused varying degrees of concern among breeders, consumers and special interest groups.

The concerns in question relate to the negative impact of breeding on the health and well-being of farmed animals. Consider two examples. First, over the last hundred years milk yield in dairy cattle has increased substantially,

from approximately 2000 kg to nearly 8000 kg per cow per annum, thanks
partly to improved management and partly to intensive breeding. This development is welcome, both from the point of view of human standards of living and
from a resource perspective. However, it has become evident that excessive
breeding for high milk yields leads to animal health problems, including
increases in digestive disorders and the incidence of mastitis, and reduced
fertility and calving performance. Second, as we indicated above, a huge
acceleration in the growth rate of broilers has been secured by modern selection
techniques. The time required for broilers to attain commercially desirable
weight has, as a result, been cut substantially. But as an unintended side-effect
the birds now suffer from severe leg problems. Over recent decades companies
involved in broiler breeding have invested considerable resources in breeding
for leg health. The problems persist, however. Some conditions have become
less common, but others have become more prevalent. In a recent Danish
study it was reported that nearly one third of the birds had a significantly
reduced ability to walk normally. There is every reason to believe that this
impairment is painful to the animals. And a number of other problems seem
to be connected directly or indirectly with accelerated growth. For example,
the parent animals used to produce eggs from which the broiler chickens are
hatched endure strict food restrictions under which they are permitted to eat
about half of what their appetite motivates them to eat. In the absence of this
restriction the animals become obese, with dramatic negative effects on both
animal welfare and production.

The genetic correlations between production and health traits appear in some
cases, then, to be unfavourable in the sense that the genes that bring increases in
productivity introduce dispositions to disease and other health problems. Even
so, carefully designed breeding programmes might allow breeders to improve
health and increase production at the same time – although the increases in production generated by programmes of the latter kind may be smaller than they
would have been if the animal health issues had been ignored. But just how
important is it to breed animals in a way that ensures good health? Are we
morally obliged to do this? Or are those who worry about the plight of animals
on modern intensive farms misguided sentimentalists? To answer questions of
this kind it is necessary to look at the ethical principles that underpin concern
about modern breeding practices directly. We shall do this in the next section.
In practical terms we also need to examine alternative development paths for
the future. We shall do this in the section after next.

Ethical limits to breeding

Ethical problems relating to breeding differ markedly from those connected
with the way animals are kept by the farmer (Sandøe *et al.*, 1999). The ethical
issues raised by animal husbandry concern *existing* animals. They include
questions about the treatment of animals, and more specifically about housing
systems, the opportunity to exercise 'normal' behaviour, the incidence of

disease and so on. Here the relevant question is roughly this: bearing in mind that some husbandry practices cause pain or discomfort, what kinds of treatment are acceptable in the efficient farming of this animal?

By contrast, ethical questions concerning farm animal breeding relate to *potential* animals. The relevant question is: what sort of animals should there be? To answer this question we need to clarify the purposes for which it is acceptable to alter the genetic composition of animals (to a greater or lesser extent) in order to improve their utility to us. And we need to ask what kinds of concern should be considered in this connection. To some observers the mere thought of intentionally changing genetic composition through breeding is ethically unacceptable. Interfering with the 'natural' selection process is 'playing God'. A more widespread and moderate attitude to breeding runs as follows. We cannot undo our earlier interventions into the animal kingdom. Farm animals are, in any case, already domesticated and recognisably distinct from their wild relatives or ancestors. So the key ethical question is not whether we should abandon animal breeding but how we should breed. In particular, we need to clarify the ethical limits of breeding.

In scientific and public debate three (as it were) auxiliary topics are repeatedly raised when modern breeding and reproductive technologies are under discussion. These are: animal welfare, animal integrity and biodiversity. Let us examine these topics, and their relevance to breeding, in turn.

The precise definition of *animal welfare* is the subject of intense scientific and philosophical discussion (Appleby and Sandøe, 2002). However, it is fair to say that both physical health and the ability to exercise a range of normal behaviours are important measures of welfare (e.g. Sandøe *et al.*, 1997), and there is widespread agreement that pain and other forms of suffering impair welfare. The welfare problems encountered in animal husbandry relate in part, as already indicated, to breeding goals connected with high levels of productivity (Christiansen and Sandøe, 2000). Turkeys bred for muscular development suffer increased leg disorders and other health problems. Male birds are sometimes too heavy to mount females without damaging them, which makes artificial insemination necessary. Clearly, these side-effects of laudable breeding goals may reduce the welfare of turkeys. Again, the breeding of double-muscled cattle for beef has led to calving difficulties. In many cases Caesarean sections are required (Broom, 1998), and this increases the risk of welfare problems. Finally, reproductive technologies can also have a negative impact on welfare. Embryo transfer makes surgery necessary in sheep and pigs, and *in vitro* fertilisation has several unintended and unwelcome results: it leads to an increased number of late, spontaneous abortions and other birth problems (McEvoy *et al.*, 2001).

Most people would readily acknowledge that animal welfare is an ethical concern with a direct bearing on the issues raised by livestock farming and farm animal breeding. Is it, however, the only such concern? An example involving laying hens suggests that it is not.

Modern egg production systems are notorious for animal welfare problems. Often the laying hens live in battery cages, with limited possibility to walk.

Alternatively, they are kept in large groups where there is a better opportunity for exercise, but this results in feather pecking, which in turn leads to damage to plumage and ultimately flesh wounds. Cruelly, these wounds encourage additional pecking from other hens, and there is in the worst cases a real risk of cannibalism.

Several attempts have been made to alter production systems to mitigate these negative effects, but they have been largely unsuccessful. A common containment measure is to mutilate day-old chickens by removing the tips of their beaks. Another approach involves breeding: it is to breed blind hens. For according to a Canadian study (Ali and Cheng, 1985), congenitally blind chickens do not face the same problems of feather pecking, cannibalism and other associated issues as sighted ones. Purely from an animal welfare perspective, the breeding and use of these hens appears to be quite unproblematic. Studies also show that the blind hens have no problem finding feed and water, have a lower feed intake, a body weight similar to laying hens with unimpaired vision, and produce more eggs per day. Even though they might miss out on some of the pleasures and joys of chicken life, it is perhaps reasonable to expect that they will adapt and lead a life that is unobjectionable from the point of view of welfare – at least, compared to the feather-pecking alternative.

Whether it really is better, for the birds' welfare, to create congenitally blind hens depends on how animal welfare is defined. Welfare may be, and often is, defined with an emphasis on the absence of disease and pain. But it may also be defined so that it involves 'good functioning' – that is, so that an essential element of it is the ability to exercise 'normal' biological capacities (normality being relative to the species). Plainly, the second of these definitions would have the implication that blindness in hens *is* a welfare problem.

But the objection to breeding congenitally blind chickens may be of a very different nature altogether. To many people the objection to breeding blind hens to ensure that they can be accommodated within an intensive production system is not about welfare. It is about *animal integrity* and its violation (Sandøe et al., 1999). How powerful is this second kind of objection?

The concept of animal integrity is difficult to define (Christiansen and Sandøe, 2000). A notion of roughly the following kind captures a widely felt worry: 'We can define the genetic integrity of the animal as the genome being left intact. This seems to be a meaningful notion in view of the fact that we can clearly point out some factors or actions by which the genome would not be left intact' (Vorstenbosch, 1993, p. 110). What does leaving the genome intact mean? One obvious way to understand this is that we should abstain from technical interference with the genome. Then this definition only covers cases in which genetic change has been brought about through gene technology, and in the case of the blind hens technology of this kind was not involved. It therefore seems that the idea that animals have a certain nature, or range of natural features (e.g. sight), is essential to the notion of animal integrity. To violate an animal's integrity, on this expanded definition, is to breed an animal in which this nature, or range of natural features, is no longer intact.

It remains to be seen whether the notion that an animal possesses an essential nature can be sustained outside a religious context – that is, without defining what is natural by reference to the intention of a creator. But the concept of integrity is not without other problems (Sandøe and Holtug, 1998). A scientific objection to the concept is that it fails to take into account the fact that genomes exhibit a high degree of plasticity within changing environments. A more philosophical objection asks whether the concern for animal integrity is about what we do to individual animals or about what we do to entire species/races. In any case the 'conservatism' involved in the whole idea of preserving existing genotypes can be questioned. What is so special about these genotypes? Returning to animal welfare for a moment, it might be asked how respect for integrity benefits the animals. Currently, broilers experience leg problems as a result of over-rapid juvenile growth, as mentioned earlier. What would justify a refusal to initiate selective breeding programmes to eliminate this problem and improve animal welfare? Would the desire to maintain the integrity of existing breeds be enough? Is it not plausible to hold that breeding for improved health and a reduction in susceptibility to naturally occurring diseases is an unconditionally good thing?

If animal integrity and animal welfare are both considered relevant, a balancing of the two concerns against each other will often be necessary. This raises further questions. Are the two concerns equally important? Is one more important than the other – or should one, ultimately, be regarded as ethically irrelevant and abandoned?

Let us turn to the third thing people worry about when they have misgivings about the modern breeding industry: *biodiversity*. Concerns about biodiversity are not about the welfare of individual animals. Nor can they be adequately captured by talk about the integrity of individual species. They focus instead on the existence and value of whole populations. And more particularly, they focus on the variation and variability of life forms, functions, structures and processes that populations embody at the species and genetic level.

The importance of biodiversity to breeders can be hard to gauge. To many in the industry, breeding is all about retaining genetic information and resources for future use. However, there are signs that the diversity of the gene pool within breeds and species is being threatened by intensive selection pressures. For example, variation within cattle has decreased following widespread use of artificial insemination in Holstein dairy cattle, where the overriding purpose has been to make a healthy breed available to farmers.

The number of extinct or endangered cattle breeds has indeed increased dramatically over recent decades. In several European countries three breeds or fewer make up more than 90% of dairy herds. Advanced breeding programmes typically focus on a limited number of breeds, discarding other, more traditional breeds. From 1970 onwards a breeding programme in Norway focusing on the Norwegian Red Cattle ensured that more than twenty-five indigenous breeds went out of production within just two decades, leaving the Norwegian Red Cattle as the only commercially viable dairy cattle breed (Christensen, 1998).

Losses of biodiversity provoke anxiety for a variety of reasons. First, and most simply, many people look upon biological diversity in itself as something that has intrinsic, or fundamental, value. Second, in countries that possess a wide variety of, say, cattle breeds, such as Norway, the loss of breeds is often regarded as destructive of the local cultural heritage. Third, some observers have speculated that if there is insufficient genetic variation within or between breeds, it will become more difficult to go back and remedy existing trait-related problems with, for example, animal welfare; and that it will be difficult to adapt breeds to new production systems and management techniques.

One way to meet these concerns would be to conserve all breeds, or at least breeds of special importance, perhaps using cryopreservation techniques. However, this is not very likely to happen at the moment: it is expensive and in any case it is unclear who (breeders? the food industry? society?) should bear the costs involved. In reality, then, priorities will have to be identified in anticipation of future needs. We will, for example, need to predict whether certain genes will become important for quality characteristics and performance at some point in the future – something easier said than done, of course.

The way forward

The main goals of twentieth century animal breeding were to produce highly productive and feed-conversion efficient livestock and to develop animals which in other ways met market demand, such as leaner pigs. However, these aims are likely to be supplemented by others in the twenty-first century. A number of changes have been apparent over the last few decades. The values we examined in the last section – animal welfare, animal integrity and biodiversity – are one of the drivers of change here. So in looking towards future trends it makes sense to ask what initiatives are being taken to deal with the ethical problems we have identified in real life.

To begin with, it is important to realise that, where most species are concerned, the breeding sector is no longer very attached to the local farming communities in Western Europe and North America. Animal breeding is an industry operating under unforgiving market forces, and in some areas, such as poultry, breeding is entirely in the hands of a very small number of multinational companies. At the same time, however, legislation governing animal protection and welfare is not international – at least, if we put aside European Union initiatives. These conditions, together with the difficulty of finding objective measures of animal welfare and exercising effective regulatory control, make it difficult to ensure that breeders address welfare-related problems.

In the Nordic countries, in framing the breeding goals of dairy cattle, efforts have been made over the past twenty-five years, to bring in traits other than those enhancing productivity: health and welfare have been included among the parameters of successful breeding. This has been financially feasible because health problems in dairy cattle give rise to economic losses stemming from treatment costs and lowered production. Thus an essentially economic motive has made it possible to combine health-related and income-related breeding aims. However, in other branches of farm animal breeding it may turn out to be much more difficult to find ways to breed for increased health and welfare that are economically attractive. This would appear to be the situation in the case of poultry, for example, where any economic losses to poulterers generated by reduced health and welfare are stubbornly offset by corresponding gains.

Breeders operate in an environment in which it is absolutely necessary to cater for ethical concerns without compromising economic competitiveness. This need is recognised in a recent, on-going EU project (2000–2003) on sustainable farm animal breeding and reproduction (Liinamo and Neeteson, 2001). This project attempts to map the concerns and priorities of various stakeholders, such as citizens in various countries around the world, animal welfare organisations, retailers, farmers and the breeding industry itself.

The notion of *sustainable* farm animal breeding cannot be defined with just one specific set of values or one specific list of moral concerns, because ethical dilemmas lie at the core of sustainable development. However, if they are pursued sensibly, discussions of sustainability that refer to animal ethics and biotechnology will open up the discussion of ethical issues and help to set an agenda. If these discussions are to be fruitful, and if sustainability is to be more than a marketing ploy or an empty rallying cry of interest groups, it will be necessary for all parties to be aware of their own priorities and the values on which these priorities are based. Equally, a meaningful discussion among stakeholders in animal breeding will require them to state their values in a transparent manner. Obviously, an open-minded attitude to other stake-holders' views will be very important in any dialogue that takes place.

Acknowledgements

We would like to thank the following members of the SEFABAR network for making valuable suggestions and comments: Gert Nieuwhof, Johan van Arendonk, Yvan Heyman, Dietmar Flock, Cliff Nixey, Manuel Carrillo, Pieter Knap and Piet Simons. We also benefited from comments and advice from Henrik Callesen, Stine B. Christiansen, Lars Gjøl Christensen and Paul Robinson. We are grateful to the European Commission for financial support.

References

Ali, A. and Cheng, K. M. (1985) Early egg production in genetically blind (rc/rc) chickens in comparison with sighted (Rc+/rc) controls, *Poultry Science* 64: 789–94.
Appleby, M.C. and Sandøe, P. 2002. Philosophical debates relevant to animal welfare: the nature of well-being. *Animal Welfare*. In press.

Broom, D.M. (1998) The effects of biotechnology on animal welfare. In Holland, A. and Johnson, A. (eds) (1997). *Animal Biotechnology and Ethics*. London: Chapman & Hall, pp. 69–82.

Christensen, L.G. (1998) Future market and consumer oriented breeding goals. *Acta Agriculturæ Scandinavica, Section A: Animal Science Supplement* 28: 45–53.

Christiansen, S.B. and Sandøe, P. 2000. Bioethics: limits to the interference with life. *Animal Reproduction Science* 60–61: 15–29.

Liinamo, A.-E. and Neeteson, A.-M. (2001) Sustainable breeding for farm animals: overview of ongoing research and business efforts in Europe. Paper presented at the 52nd Annual Meeting of the EAAP, Budapest, 26–29 August 2001, pp. 1–6. http://www.sefabar.org/publication.htm.

McEvoy, T.G., Robinson, J.J. and Sinclair, K.D. (2001) Developmental consequences of embryo and cell manipulation in mice and farm animals. *Reproduction* 122: 507–18.

Sandøe, P. and Holtug, N. (1998) Ethical aspects of biotechnology in farm animal production. *Acta Agriculturæ Scandinavica, Section A: Animal Science Supplement* 29: 51–8.

Sandøe, P., Crisp, R. and Holtug, N. (1997) Ethics. In: Appleby, M.C. and Hughes, B. (eds) *Animal Welfare*. Wallingford: C.A.B. International, pp. 3–17.

Sandøe, P., Nielsen, B.L., Christensen, L.G. and Sørensen, P. (1999) Staying good while playing God – the ethics of breeding farm animals. *Animal Welfare* 8: 313–28.

Thibier, M. and Wagner, H.-G. (2002) World statistics for artificial insemination in cattle. *Livestock Production Science* 74: 203–12.

Vorstenbosch, J. (1993) The concept of integrity: its significance for the ethical discussion on biotechnology and animals. *Livestock Production Science* 36: 109–12.

Further reading

Holland, A. and Johnson, A. (eds) 1997. *Animal Biotechnology and Ethics*. London: Chapman & Hall.

Sandøe, P., Nielsen, B.L., Christensen, L.G. and Sørensen, P. 1999. Staying good while playing God – the ethics of breeding farm animals. *Animal Welfare* 8: 313–28.

Biography

Christian Gamborg has a PhD from the Royal Veterinary and Agricultural University and is a research scientist at the Danish Forest and Landscape Research Institute and at the Centre for Bioethics and Risk Assessment. His research interests include ethics, sustainability and biodiversity in relation to land use, forest and natural resource management.

Peter Sandøe was educated at the University of Copenhagen and at the University of Oxford. From 1992 to 1997 he was Head of the Bioethics Research Group at the University of Copenhagen. He is now Research Professor in Bioethics at the Royal Veterinary and Agricultural University in Copenhagen and director of a newly established interdisciplinary Centre for Bioethics and Risk Assessment. Since 1992 he has served as Chairman of the Danish Ethical Council for Animals and president of the European Society for Agricultural and Food Ethics.

15 Farm animal welfare

Joyce D'Silva

Do animals suffer?

In 1984 Peter Roberts, the founder of Compassion in World Farming (CIWF), took a court case against a farm in Sussex where veal calves were being kept in narrow wooden crates, unable to turn round for most of their lives. Peter claimed that the calves were suffering, as they could not walk, could not socialise and were also in an unhealthy state as they were being fed a low-iron liquid-only diet, totally lacking the fibre which calves need from two weeks of age.

These particular calves were owned by a community of monks. One of the senior monks told the press he couldn't see what all the media fuss was about as animals couldn't suffer.

The case was lost, and lost again on appeal. Just a couple of years later, the then government announced that this system of rearing calves was going to be banned – and banned it was in the UK from 1 January 1990.

It may well seem obvious to most of us that animals with legs need to walk, birds with wings to fly. We tread on a dog's paw and he yelps – obviously in pain. Do we really have to prove that animals suffer? And, if so, how can we do this?

How do we define suffering? Perhaps sometimes it's just the awareness of physical pain. We seem to differentiate, though, between short-lived physical pain – 'I've got a rotten stomach ache' – and long-term painful conditions – 'she suffers so much with her arthritis'. Is a stomach ache not really in the suffering category because we know from experience that it will almost certainly pass? Of course, an animal with stomach ache might not know this, so is it, therefore, possible that in such a situation the animal would be suffering more?

We know that suffering is often not related to physical pain at all – it is to do with our emotions, relationships, families and jobs (or lack of jobs). We all prefer to be in a 'happy' state. And although for each of us happiness will be attained in different ways, there may well be common factors – the feeling of good relationships with others around one, be they partners, parents, children, colleagues or friends, a feeling of being in a comfortable or stimulating environment, round the hearth or on the mountainside, for example. Basic comfort needs will have been met – we will not be desperately hungry, nor too cold or hot. Our bodies will be able to move comfortably, whether we are hill walking, cycling or stretching out on a cushion. We will not be afraid or feel threatened physically or emotionally. Everything will seem right. In fact, mild mental suffering may arrive only when we suddenly realise 'this can't last forever' – and the awareness of change and loss of the magic moment may fleetingly or completely dull it.

Of course, what I have just written is pure guess work. I cannot ever know with certainty your joy, nor you mine. With intimacy, I can be fairly sure I understand how another human feels – but I can never be quite, quite certain. It is impossible to be 'inside' another's mind or heart.

Equally, when I see an apparently happy animal, I can only conjecture as to its state of mind. I can know if it's in a comfortable environment, or if it's well fed and watered. I can appraise myself of its possibilities for socialising with its own kind or, as with pet dogs, with human substitutes. The animal appears happy – the dog wags her tail, the cat purrs, the pony whinnies, the cow chews the cud in contentment in the evening sun. Surely, surely these animals are happy. As far as I can ever know.

So what then is suffering? Is it the absence of happiness? Is it when I'm hungry, thirsty, too cold, too hot, overworked, uncomfortable, in pain? Surely these factors will contribute to a likely state of suffering. But often it is in the emotional states that I find my greatest happiness and likewise endure my greatest suffering. If my relationships with family, partner, friend(s) or colleague(s) are either non-existent or in a disturbed state, no amount of physical comfort or good food will make me happy. And part of those poor relationships would be the awful yearning for them to be better – for life to be other than it is.

Could it be likewise for animals? Kept in poor environments or hungry, thirsty, too cold, too hot, they appear to suffer. Common sense tells me they *do* suffer. But for them, too, are the social relationships crucial? If their natural families/flock/herd groups are torn apart, will they not feel that something is amiss in their world?

In the farm animal world, and indeed in the 'domesticated' or 'captive' animal world generally, our assumptions are complicated by the fact that the animal we observe is perhaps very different from its wild ancestors. But – just a moment – so are you and I! Yet, under our veneers of civilisation and our social and cultural conditioning, there are surely the primal emotions, beating away.

A few hundred years ago it was almost expected that some of your children would die young. Now, in the West, we find it hard to come to terms with the death of one child. But in countries where poverty and infectious diseases still kill many children, their deaths may seem to be accepted almost fatalistically by their parents. I would argue that in both situations this fatalism is simply a coping mechanism – just as the doctor or nurse cuts off emotionally from the suffering and death of their patients. The emotions are still there – but to indulge in them could make life unbearable. Could this also be the case for our farm animals?

Take a two-day old calf away from his mother. He will cry for her and be obviously upset. His need to suckle from her and be with her is not being met. His world has been turned upside down in an instant. The calf is taken away so his mother can produce milk for us instead. The price of milk you could say. But the price society is prepared to pay. In ignorance?

Take the breeding sow. Until a couple of years ago nearly a quarter of a million sows in the UK were kept in narrow, metal barred stalls, unable to turn round throughout their sixteen-week pregnancies. Some were actually chained to the floor. The sow stall/tether system.

Animal behaviourists tell us interesting things about pigs – but most of all they tell us how intelligent they are – more intelligent than dogs. A pig learns to operate a computer more quickly than a dog (if that is a mark of intelligence!). If you or I kept a pregnant bitch in a narrow cage, unable to turn round throughout her (much shorter) pregnancy, perhaps chained to the floor, we would be prosecuted.

Double standards in society. Based on what? A fairly long tradition of 'pet' dogs and an equally long tradition of 'farm animals' or 'food animals'. As if the object of the animal's life (imposed by us, of course) is sufficient justification for treating it in an abysmal way.

This huge anomaly in the way we categorise different species of animals is hard to justify in any rational way. We endlessly petition governments in the Far East to ban the killing of dogs or cats for food, yet we happily confine hens in cages to produce eggs and keep chickens and pigs in foul conditions to produce meat for our own dinner tables. There is no logic here. There may be some ethical imperialism. If it's wrong to kill a dog for one's dinner, what makes it right to kill a lamb?

Thanks to an excellent public and political campaign, led by Compassion in World Farming in the late 1980s and early 1990s, the cruel sow stall system has been banned in the UK and is on its way out in the European Union. Sadly, it's the norm in American hog farms and growing apace in countries like China, which are accepting the very factory farming methods we in the West are rejecting.

But wait a minute. Even our British sows don't escape the crate altogether. As farrowing (giving birth) time approaches, the sow is moved into another metal barred, concrete floored crate – the farrowing crate. Here she gives birth and suckles her piglets for four weeks.

We have selectively bred pigs to make them prolific. Sows are now larger and heavier than they used to be (around a quarter of a tonne) and produce more piglets than they have teats for the piglets to suckle from. The not surprising result is more small and weak piglets which are at risk of dying or being crushed.

So when pig breeders tell us that what is good about farrowing crates is that they stop the sow lying on her piglets, the first response is – of course, she's so immobilised she *can't* lie on them. But we need to ask some more fundamental questions like: why are sows so huge and cumbersome? Why are there so many piglets? Why are so many piglets small and weak? Why do so many die anyway?

What's bad about farrowing crates? Well, in her natural environment (light woodland) the sow builds a large nest of twigs and leaves, maybe more than a couple of metres high, in which she gives birth and suckles her piglets. The nest keeps them warm and safe from predators. The sow will defend it fiercely.

A minority of pig farmers have already switched from farrowing crates to alternative, more humane systems. Some use well-bedded outdoor arcs where the sow can farrow and suckle; others use indoor, straw-based systems. The straw factor is so obviously important to the sow. It helps her fulfil her nest-building instinct.

At this time, just before farrowing, the nest-building urge is particularly strong. Watch the sow in the farrowing crate – she makes repetitive down, forward and up movements with her snout as she builds her phantom nest. In reality, her only physical contact is with the harsh metal bars and concrete floor of her prison. She may be given a few handfuls of sawdust or straw to soften the discomfort.

This sow is not, probably, in physical pain though the border line between discontent and pain is a narrow one. But every innate urge in her is being frustrated. Is this not suffering? And when her piglets are removed from her at 3–4 weeks of age, is she not distressed at this ruthless kidnap? She would normally suckle them for 3–4 months.

Something is amiss. Her social relationships have been violated and her nurturing instincts unfulfilled. We have refused to acknowledge her motherhood. So ironic in a society which now pays at least lip service to the rights of the pregnant woman to give birth in the environment of her choosing and encourages and helps her to suckle her newborn infant.

How strange too that we have banned the crate for the pregnant sow, but kept it in place for the farrowing sow. How inconsistent is our concern! But I didn't know, they say, maybe you say.

Is ignorance of cruelty a valid excuse for supporting it? Possibly, if the information is not in the public domain. If I buy a product, totally unaware that it is manufactured by a company operating with slave labour (but actually not making that knowledge public), I can be excused. How could I have known?

But the information about cruel farming systems is there in the public arena – you need only contact CIWF or the Royal Society for the Prevention of Cruelty to Animals (RSPCA) or log on to their websites to find out everything you might wish to know about how farm animals are reared, transported and slaughtered.

We might all acknowledge a duty of care towards those animals actually in our care – be they pets or farm animals – but do we have a duty of remote care for the animals whom we end up eating or wearing or whose mammary or ovarian products (milk and eggs) we also consume? We, or many of us, now try to buy ethical – or at least not obviously unethical – products. We may boycott cheap goods made in the Far East, being uncertain about the workers' conditions, we may buy our tea and coffee from fair traders, we may question if our new carpet or rug was made by child labour – but do we enquire how our animal products were produced?

Did that chicken leg on my plate provide the total support for a broiler chicken whose other leg was crippled through carrying around a vastly over-weight torso? The meat (broiler) chicken now reaches slaughter weight in just six weeks – half the time it took him 30 years ago. He's been selectively bred to grow incredibly fast and put on lots of (more valuable) breast meat.

As a result his legs can't cope. Every year millions of chickens in the UK spend the last week or two of their short lives in pain, sometimes severe pain, as they hobble past their companions (17 or more of them to a square metre of floor space) to reach food and water. The mortality rate of these fast-growing meat chickens is seven times that of egg-laying breeds of the same age, accord-ing to the EU's Scientific Committee on Animal Health and Animal Welfare. This same committee declared in 2000: 'Most of the welfare issues that relate specifically to commercial broiler production are a direct consequence of genetic selection for faster and more efficient production of chicken meat' (SCAHAW, 2000).

Not only do we deprive animals of their natural familial relationships and keep them confined and overcrowded, but we actually breed them to have unsustainable bodies. Those chickens don't reach puberty until they're 18 weeks old. As things stand right now, probably only a quarter of the 800+ million chickens we rear each year in the UK could sustain their lives to reach puberty – if they were allowed to.

But – they tell us – they don't *need* to reach puberty. They're slaughtered at six weeks old! True – yet in my gut I know there is something fundamentally corrupt about a system which breeds an animal which is physiologically incap-able of reaching even its own puberty, never mind old age/natural death.

If you think logically, you realise some of those chickens have to live long enough to breed new chickens. So how do they do it? By starvation. The breeding flocks of broilers get short rations – this slows down the fast growth rate so that the birds can live to puberty and breed.

With turkeys we've gone even a further step. The modern selectively bred turkey is now so huge, so cumbersome compared to his wild cousins and ancestors that the male cannot be relied on to mount the female – or to do so without damaging her. So he is 'milked' for his semen instead.

It is a strange society which abhors bestiality, but employs people to mastur-
bate turkey cocks on a regular basis so that artificial insemination can take place
and we can all celebrate the birthday of the Prince of Peace with the corpse of
an animal which probably never knew a moment's real peace.

Can it be ethical to rear an animal – or rather millions of them every year –
who can no longer mate by natural means because of what we've done to them?

Selective breeding for excessive muscle has been taken to the extreme in the
breeding of huge meaty cattle of a breed called 'Belgian Blues'. The breeders
latched on to a 'natural' mutation in a gene which produced 'double-muscled'
animals. Now these mighty creatures with their enormous hind-quarters are
highly prized, as you get so much meat off one animal. The down side is
that the females don't have a sufficiently expanding pelvic region to be able
to give birth to their double-muscled calves, and most births are by Caesarean
(SCAHAW, 2001).

A woman can choose to have a caesarean or is offered one because normal
birth might prove difficult or dangerous. For the Belgian Blue cow, there's
usually no choice – so the discomfort, post-operative pain and general distress
of a Caesarean must be endured. She knows not why.

These huge frustrations, mutilations and interferences that we impose on
farm animals are perhaps all the more reprehensible *because* they do not know
why they take place.

The pregnant pig does not know why she can't walk or turn round or has to
lie on her excrement and concrete. The farrowing sow does not know why she
can find no building materials with which to build her nest. She doesn't know
why her piglets are taken away so early, when her urge is still to mother them.

The limping broiler chicken doesn't know why he is so uncomfortable, why
it has to be so painful to drag his legs over to the feed and water. The breeding
chicken doesn't know why she's so constantly hungry – she just *is*.

And, of course, new methods of exploitation emerge constantly. We can now
perform embryo transfers on cows and other farm animals. Embryos are
extracted from one cow and implanted in another. The raison d'être is, of
course, financial. You take a high quality cow and inject her with hormones
to induce super-ovulation (releasing lots of extra egg cells from her ovaries).
You then artificially inseminate her with high quality bull's semen, wait a few
days, then remove the tiny embryos and implant them in the uterus of some
low quality cows, who act as surrogate mothers and bring the embryos to
term. The whole messy business was initially done by straight abdominal
surgery; now embryos and eggs are implanted and extracted via the cervix.
However, it is not without pain – as the cow's cervix is only 'open' when
she is on heat. In fact, the procedure is so painful that the law of the land
requires an epidural anaesthetic injection to be given into the spinal cord.
(When embryo transfer is done on sheep and pigs, surgery is usually required.)

The high quality cow is now freed up from having to endure a nine-month
pregnancy, and can swiftly be 'used' again to release yet more of those precious
egg cells.

It is one thing to transplant an ordinary embryo – but how about a genetically engineered or cloned one? For this may be the future of farming, they tell us.

Cloning sits neatly alongside selective breeding and embryo transfer – and is based on the simple premise that best is best. So you take a cell from a 'best' animal and clone it to produce lots of replicas. Of course, along the way you have to insert your cloned embryo via cervical interference or surgery into another of those useful surrogate mums. Worse still, cloned animals have a quirky way of growing too big in the borrowed uterus – so Caesareans are often required. Various scientists have calculated the mortality rates for farm animal clones. It is fair to say that around half of all cloned farm animals die shortly before or soon after birth (Wilmut *et al.*, 1998; Renard *et al.*, 1999; Pennisi and Vogel, 2000).

These poor results seem generally predictable. Genetic engineering is the cutting edge of breeding for best. By inserting genes (or deleting genes), the animal is designed to fulfil a particular niche: a cow producing milk which makes great cheese, goats producing milk which contains a spider silk protein – useful for manufacturing bullet-proof vests they tell us – or just plain old faster-growing, leaner pigs, cattle and sheep.

Genetic engineering too has a poor success rate, with animals born with multiple defects, like the first-ever genetically engineered pigs (the Beltsville pigs) whose extra human or cattle growth hormone genes made them unable to stand up or mate. It has not got a lot better since (Jaenisch, 2002).

But all these (ab)uses of farm animals raise those key fundamental ethical questions about what our relationship with them should be – apart from the relationship of buying their meat/milk/eggs, cooking them and eating them.

Is it right to keep animals in systems where natural behaviours are impossible? Is it right to overfeed or underfeed animals so that they grow at the rate that suits us (broiler chickens and broiler chicken breeding birds)? Is it right to take the young away from their mothers (dairy calves at one day, piglets at 3–4 weeks, chickens from the moment of egg laying)? Is it right to keep animals in isolation (breeding sows, dairy/veal calves) or overcrowded conditions (broiler chickens, fattening pigs)?

Is it acceptable to selectively breed, clone or genetically engineer creatures who can't even survive to their own puberty, let alone old age (broiler chickens)? Or creatures whose birth requires a Caesarean? Is it all right to invade the uterus via the vagina and cervix to extract/implant embryos?

The answer to all these questions will depend on one's view of the nature and intrinsic value of the human being as opposed to the animal being. Western society – and indeed most human societies – have awarded primacy to the human, i.e. to ourselves. We can at least be certain of the intrinsic 'self-ishness' of humans everywhere.

Religion has played a key role in promoting and maintaining this distinct understanding of the human, e.g. Catholicism, which allots a soul to the human but not the animal, and the whole Judaeo-Christian tradition which holds that animals are there as an aid and benefit to humans and which we have a right to use – and, possibly, a duty to care for. However, both the Bible ('Are not five sparrows sold for two farthings, and not one of them is forgotten before God?', Luke 12: 6) and the Islamic holy book, the Qur'an ('there is not an animal on earth, nor a bird that flies on its wings, but they are communities like you', 6. 33) do intimate that God *values* the animal creation.

Even traditional Hinduism, whilst accepting karma-based reincarnation of souls (possibly including animals) has lived for many years alongside a tradition of animal sacrifice to appease the god/desses. Only Buddhism and Jainism have awarded an intrinsic value to animals, regarding them as sentient beings (along-side humans).

In the West the important point about our majority religious tradition is that it has totally permeated Western culture. Although a majority of the inheritors of the Judaeo-Christian tradition have rejected religious practice, and in many cases have rejected belief in an almighty God, society as a whole still uses much of the traditional religious view of human primacy in its dealings with animals. This is an anomaly which requires serious questioning.

If the religious anthropocentric view is rejected, then we have to look at other justifications for human primacy. It may be easy to make a case on grounds of intellectual supremacy, rather less easy on grounds of technological expertise (designing a computer versus designing a honeycomb – there may not be much in it).

If you take the really reductionist view and put it all down to genetics and cellular development, we tend to come out rather similar to animals too.

If modern biology has taught us anything it is surely that humans and animals are incredibly similar, both genetically and physiologically, but also emotionally. It was, after all, Darwin who declared that 'man and the higher animals, especially the primates, have some few instincts in common. All have the same senses, intuitions, and sensations, similar passions, affections and emotions . . . they feel wonder and curiosity . . . they possess the same faculties of imitation, attention, deliberation, choice, memory, imagination, the association of ideas, and reason though in very different degrees' (Darwin, 1871).

As for emotional supremacy, it is hard to see how human emotions of anger, rage and greed which sometimes lead to mass murders (wars) are in any way superior to the tiger killing one creature for his dinner, or even to a fox getting high on a chicken-house bloodbath.

If we award intrinsic value to human beings – and a bevy of international and national laws make it clear that we do – then it is hard to see how one can make a good case for *not* awarding intrinsic value to animals. Our similarities at every level so obviously outweigh our differences.

If we believe our lives have purpose and meaning, then can we deny this to animals? Many humans may live 'good' lives, without ever giving intellectual time to pondering such purpose and meaning. They have simply *lived.* Likewise animals may not consider the purpose and meaning of their lives – they simply live them, making choices as they go. As with humans, most of their choices will be for their own (or their kin's) benefit. It is hard to argue that a pig's life is less important to it than mine is to me. We both seek happiness/pleasure/well-being, though in different ways.

Already society is moving forward on this issue. In 1997 all the member states of the EU added a legally binding protocol to the European Treaty, recognising that animals are indeed 'sentient beings', i.e. that they can feel pain and can suffer.

But, if we are so similar to animals, from where *do* we get the right to selectively breed them, alter their genetic structure, keep them in cages and crates, transport them long distances and genetically engineer or clone them?

If we reject the religious tradition of human primacy and supremacy, we are left with a fairly inadequate tool-kit to justify such actions, one which states plainly: we are intellectually superior/we have always done it. But dominance on its own is a somewhat Fascist 'ethic' on which to base our relationship with other sentient beings.

If you feel that the ways in which we exploit animals in intensive farming are unacceptable, you may feel that for farming to be acceptable the animals must be kept in decent conditions, free-range preferably, be fed a natural diet, and be able to mix with their own kind, and that mothers should be allowed to suckle for a natural period, and that no animal be kept in isolation or overcrowding. Some farmers are trying to do all these things – to give the animals real quality of life before death.

For many of us, this is the acceptable answer – we want to eat meat but really don't want any animals to suffer during their lives. Animal welfare campaigners are working to achieve these high welfare standards for all farm animals.

It seems that once people become aware of the kind of suffering inherent in factory-type farming, they do want to abandon its products. The huge increase in free-range egg sales is the first tangible and weighty proof of this. Already, two major retailers in the UK – Marks and Spencer and Waitrose – have stopped selling battery eggs and sell only free-range eggs. This is clearly in response to consumer demand, which in itself was accompanied by vigorous campaigning and lobbying by organisations like CIWF.

Organic farmers may be leading the way in their use of outdoor – or indoor, bedded – systems and in their refusal to use embryo transfer or genetic engineering, but farmers generally are becoming more aware of animal welfare as an issue. Farming 'bodies' now engage in dialogue with organisations like CIWF and the RSPCA.

But, people ask, can kinder farming feed the world? Surely the answer to global hunger is global productivity? This question alone raises a plethora of others – not least about the *real* costs of intensive animal production. These costs include environmental degradation, loss of genetic diversity, increase of agri-business operations at the expense of the small farmer, inappropriately high capital investment, high resource use of factory farms in developing countries, and the feeding of human-edible grains and legumes to farm animals to produce unaffordable meat with an overall loss of protein/calories.

We are rearing more and more farm animals but on fewer farms. Pig numbers in the EU have nearly doubled in the last thirty years (European Parliament, 1999), but the *number* of pig farms has more than halved (Boschma *et al.*, 1999). A 1999 EU Commission report on agriculture and the environment comments: 'The large number of pigs per hectare may have a high impact on the environment in some regions of the EU. Air and soil especially need constant protection against the negative influences of intensification' (ibid.).

By 1996 43% of the world's meat was being produced in intensive systems, according to a report by the FAO, World Bank and USAID (Haan *et al.*, 1996). In the US such factory farms are called CAFOs – Concentrated Animal Feeding Operations.

Nearly three-quarters of the agricultural land in the EU is used to produce animal feed – globally one-third of the world's grain is grown to feed farm animals. Growing these animal feedstuffs has led to intensive monoculture crop production, and huge inputs of fertiliser and pesticide (over 450 active chemical ingredients are approved as pesticides in the UK alone) (Williams, 1999).

Pesticide use is associated with declining numbers of wild birds, loss of habitat and biodiversity, and pollution of water. More farm animals means more slurry to pollute ground water and more ammonia and methane emissions, contributing to acidification and global warming. In 1997 the journal *British Poultry Science* carried an article which declared: 'Livestock buildings are a major anthropogenic source of atmospheric pollutants, such as ammonia, nitrous oxide, methane and carbon dioxide, which contribute to soil acidification and global warming' (Wathes *et al.*, 1997).

Farm animals convert plant proteins to edible animal protein at a low efficiency rate – from 8% to 30–40%. Worse still, 87% of the fresh water consumed worldwide is used for agriculture, much of it for growing animal feed, whilst water tables fall and water scarcity increases (Pimental *et al.*, 1997).

Lester Brown, a global authority on agriculture and food issues and founder of the World Watch Institute, wrote in 1999 that for ten billion people to eat a 'US diet' (high in animal products) we would need four planets the size of the Earth to grow the extra 9 billion tonnes of grain required to feed the animals (Brown, 1999). Some may conclude that a reliance on meat will not only fail to feed the world, but may increase hunger and ruin the environment.

But, there is, of course, the final question – do we have the right to kill animals for our food and other purposes?

Society has conditioned us all, in our various social and cultural ways, to accept all sorts of ideas as received wisdom or tradition. But it is hard to accept an ethical justification for any behaviour or system just because 'that's what we've always done!'. The slave traders and opponents of women's suffrage said that. But we've moved on.

Can we put aside our conditioned reflexes and our historical association with meat eating, and take a fresh look at a piece of meat? It is dead. Some living being somewhere had its throat cut to provide a dinner for us and a living for its owners. You may be a pacifist, or believe in the Just War, but we have no war with sheep and cows. Millions of healthy vegetarians and vegans are evidence that we don't *need* to eat dead animals (or the products of living ones) to survive.

Our ethics fail us perhaps because they are 'our' ethics, anthropocentric at their core. We want to eat meat – ergo animals must be killed. We want to eat cheap meat – ergo animals are factory farmed. We want to eat kindly produced meat – ergo some animals are reared in more humane, free-range systems.

We have failed to address our supremacy and dominance. We have not questioned its *ground*. We have simply accepted its history, its tradition. In doing so, we have failed millions of sentient beings who daily suffer for our cuisine.

Our ethics are only beginning to deal with the worst aspects of factory farming – the cages, chains and crates. We have hardly begun to tackle the issue of selective breeding, and the cloning and genetic engineering of farm animals. Cost–benefit analyses are always weighted in favour of perceived human benefit. We have blinded ourselves – or maybe just failed to see – the knock-on effects for fellow humans and the planet: the increasing environmental pollution, the loss of livelihood for small farmers worldwide, the basically unsustainable nature of intensive farming.

If the human is supreme by some divine or evolutionary process, and if part of our 'supremacy' is our ability *to have ethics*, then surely it is really incumbent on us to involve those ethics in our relationship with animals, and not just draw a protective line around our nearest and dearest – or our own country, race or species?

References

Boschma, M., Joaris, A. and Vidal, C. (1999) *Concentration of Livestock Production*, in Directorate General VI, Directorate General XI and Eurostat, *Agriculture and the Environment* (www.europa.eu.int/comm/dg06/envir/).

Brown, Lester (Ed.) (1999) State of the World. A Worldwatch Institute Report on Progress Toward a Sustainable Society. Earthscan Publications Ltd., London.

Darwin, C. (1871) *The Descent of Man and Selection in Relation to Sex.*

European Parliament (1999) Europe's Deficit in Compound Feedingstuffs and Agenda 2000. *Agriculture, Forestry and Rural Development Series, Working Document*, AGRI-110 (February).

Haan, C. de, Steinfeld, H. and Blackburn, H. (1996) *Livestock and the Environment: Finding a Balance*. A study co-ordinated by the Food and Agriculture Organisation, the US Agency for International Development, the World Bank and European Commission.

Jaenisch, Rudolf, Professor of Biology at the Whitehead Institute with MIT, *CNN* 'Q&A' Programme, 4 January 2002.

Pennisi, E. and Vogel, G. (2000) Clones; a hard act to follow, *Science* 288: 1722–7.

Pimental, D., Houser, J., Preiss, E., White, O., Fang, H., Mesnick, L., Barsky, T., Tariche, S., Schreck, J. and Alpert, S. (1997) Water resources: agriculture, the environment and society. *Bioscience* 42: 97–106.

Renard, J.-P., Chastant, S., Chesné, P., Richard, C., Marchal, J., Cordonnier, N., Chavatte, P., Vignon, X. (1999) Lymphoid hypoplasia and somatic cloning, *Lancet* 353: 1489–91.

Scientific Committee on Animal Health and Animal Welfare (SCAHAW) (2000) *The Welfare of Chickens Kept for Meat Production (Broilers)*. European Commission, Health and Consumer Protection Directorate-General (March).

Scientific Committee on Animal Health and Animal Welfare (SCAHAW) (2001) *The Welfare of Cattle Kept for Beef Production*. European Commission, Health and Consumer Protection Directorate-General (April).

Wathes, C.M., Holden, M.R., Sneath, R.W., White, R.P. and Phillips, V.R. (1997) Concentrations and emission rates of aerial ammonia, nitrous oxide, methane, carbon dioxide, dust and endotoxin in UK broiler and layer houses, *British Poultry Science* 38: 14–28.

Williams, P. (1999) The use of pesticides, in a report from the Environment Agency, State of the Environment (www.environment-agency.gove.uk/s-enviro/).

Wilmut, I., Young, L. and Campbell, K.H.S. (1998) Embryonic and somatic cell cloning, *Reproduction, Fertility and Development* 10: 639–43.

Biography

Joyce D'Silva has been Chief Executive of Compassion in World Farming (CIWF), the leading international organisation campaigning against factory farming, since 1991. Joyce has authored reports on several aspects of farm animal welfare from dairy cows to genetic engineering. She has also contributed to three books on genetic engineering and has addressed the issue at venues ranging from the Cambridge Union to the European Parliament's Intergroup on Animal Welfare. She also edits CIWF's flagship magazine, *Farm Animal Voice*. She says her personal aim is to end factory farming throughout the world, preferably in her lifetime!

Part VII
Animals for medical experiments

16 The case for the use of animals in medical experiments

Mark Matfield

History of the use of animals in medical experiments

The use of animals in medical experiments dates back to the origins of scientific medicine. The very first people to inquire into the structure and function of the human body probably used animals as models. In approximately 500 BC Alcmaeon of Croton demonstrated the function of the optic nerve by cutting through it in living animals and showing that blindness resulted (Maehle and Trohler, 1987). The ancient Greek and Roman schools of medicine appear to have used animal experiments extensively to investigate basic physiology. Galen of Pergamon (130–201 AD), physician to the Roman emperor Marcus Aurelius, described many new techniques for dissecting living animals to study the function of different parts of their bodies. Whilst the dissection of conscious animals would be condemned today as the worst kind of cruelty, we should remember that different moral standards were applied in Roman times. The prevailing Stoic philosophy viewed animals as being without reason or soul and thus as mere objects.

The use of live animal dissection in anatomical demonstrations began again in the medical schools of sixteenth-century Italy and spread throughout Europe in the following century (Maehle and Trohler, 1987). Many of the most fundamental discoveries in physiology came from animal experiments, including William Harvey's demonstration of blood circulation in 1628, Robert Hooke's discovery of the function of the lungs in 1667 and Stephen Hales measurement of blood pressure in 1733 (Rhodes, 1985). As the use of animal experimentation became more common in medical research, there also arose concern, amongst its practitioners in the UK, about the suffering involved. Marshall Hall, whose work on animals and patients is credited with advancing the understanding of blood circulation, published the first set of principles for regulating animal experiments in 1831. His five principles included not using animals where the results could be obtained by another method, proper experimental design, avoiding the unnecessary repetition of animal experiments, minimising any suffering inflicted upon the animal and the proper recording of results so as to remove any necessity for repetition (Manuel, 1987).

In the United Kingdom, before the introduction of general anaesthesia in the late 1860s, medical scientists showed an increasing reluctance to perform surgical experiments on animals. In 1863 an editorial about animal experiments in the *Lancet* said: 'perhaps some two or three, or at most six, scientific men in London are known to be pursuing certain lines of investigation which require them occasionally during the course of a year to employ living animals for the purpose of their inquiries' (Anon, 1863). As a result, experimental physiology in the UK was quite underdeveloped by comparison with the rest of Europe. However, with the advent of chloroform and ether for anaesthesia, this situation began to change. Government statistics show that the number of animal experiments conducted in the UK increased from 250 in 1881 (the first year that records were kept) to 95,000 in 1910 (French, 1975).

It is a matter of scientific record that several of the most important medical advances of the twentieth century were the result of animal experimentation. The discovery and purification of insulin by Banting, Best, Macleod and Collip in 1921 is perhaps the most famous example. The crucial experiment involved making a dog diabetic by removing its pancreas and then showing that injections of a semi-purified extract of the pancreas could reverse the condition. The further purification of insulin to a point where it could be given safely to humans required numerous tests on rabbits, as this was the only method of detecting insulin activity (Bliss, 1983). Although Alexander Fleming first discovered penicillin in 1929, it was not until 1940, when Chain and Florey showed that injections of it protected mice that had been given an otherwise lethal dose of virulent bacteria, that the full potential of penicillin was discovered (Florey, 1953). Today this 'mouse protection test' still remains the essential test for antibiotics.

Since ether and chloroform are quite dangerous, longer and more complex surgery depended on the development of safer general anaesthetics. Since the essential test for anaesthetics is that they safely render animals unconscious and allow them to recover, it is not surprising that every modern anaesthetic was developed by animal experiments (Research Defence Society, undated). The list of medical advances that depended on animal experimentation is lengthy and includes many vaccines, most pharmaceutical drugs, the heart–lung machine used for open-heart surgery, the coronary bypass operation, cardiac pacemakers and organ transplantation (Gay, 1987). Indeed some have argued that essentially every important medical advance has depended on animal experiments.

It is important to record that this interpretation has been challenged by groups opposed to animal experimentation. Many of these organisations have asserted that clinical research was far more important in many or all of these developments and that the role of animal experiments has been deliberately overstated by supporters of animal experimentation (Sharpe, 1988). Indeed, much of the public debate concerning animal experimentation has focused on the question of the necessity of using it in medical science, although it would be misleading to suggest that there has been a full debate on this point.

Do we have the right to use animals for medical science?

Given that we have used animals in medical science and safety testing for so long and to such substantial benefit for humanity, does this mean that we have a right to use them in this way? To answer this question, we need to consider what constitutes a 'right'. There are several rights that we generally accord to people about which there would be little debate, including the right to life, to liberty, to freedom of expression and so forth. However, these rights are generally regarded as having concomitant responsibilities or duties. If people have a right to life, then others also have a responsibility to not kill them. If people have a right to liberty, we have a responsibility to not infringe that right. It is worth noting that these rights and responsibilities are generally limited by other factors – thus we tend to deprive people of their liberty if they are found to be a danger to others in society.

How far do rights extend? Do we have a right to an education? Surely. Do we have a right to wear clothes? This seems less like a right. Do we have a right to drive a car? Or how about the right to watch television, or the right to compose music, or to paint, or sing? The only way in which one could reasonably argue that one had a right to carry out these activities would be as an aspect of a right to act as we see fit. However, it would be extremely difficult to construct a realistic argument that supports the proposition that people have a right to carry out any of these specific activities.

So how could we argue that we have a right to experiment on animals? It seems to me that this is outside the sphere of rights. To deny someone something that they have a right to have is to deny them something that is intrinsic or important to their nature or existence. This cannot be said about animal experimentation.

It could be argued that people have a right to freedom of inquiry, in that human beings are innately inquisitive. This argument might be extended to include the right to freedom of research investigation. However, so many other aspects of human existence restrict the ability to exercise this supposed right that it seems a poor candidate for such a description.

So, if we do not have a right to experiment on animals, how should we consider this activity? It is perhaps best described as a privilege. It is an activity that is not banned or morally proscribed, but it is also not an activity that should be conducted lightly or irresponsibly. Rights-based ethics does not seem to be a very useful tool for considering the ethics of animal experimentation. It would only really permit one of two conclusions – either we have the right to do it or we do not. Utilitarian ethics is a far more useful way to consider this issue, since it allows us to balance subtle aspects of the costs and benefits of a particular animal experiment or programme of experimentation.

Contributions – setting the terms of the debate

If we reject the idea that rights have any role to play in this matter, we should consider the utilitarian approach to the ethics of animal experimentation. This has been argued both ways. Singer extends the utilitarian analysis to include animals on the grounds that they are capable of experiencing pain and suffering (Singer, 1976). From this he concludes that it is wrong for humans to cause animals pain and suffering in experiments because, by doing so, we are reducing the total amount of well-being or happiness amongst humans and animals. Does this utilitarian analysis make sense? Should the net be cast so wide as to include in the equation all animals capable of any suffering?

A more traditional utilitarian approach only considers the well-being or happiness of human beings. In its simplest sense, this type of utilitarian analysis would only take into account the distress that might be caused to humans by witnessing animal experimentation and would completely ignore any animal suffering when assessing the negative side of the equation. Can we ignore animal suffering completely in our ethical considerations?

There is one other important question to ask about the ethics of animal experimentation: how do most normal people consider the ethics of this matter? It seems to me that this type of question is very rarely asked. Most philosophy works deductively. It starts with a premise and then draws conclusions about what this means for human actions, our existence, or whatever. Granted, most of the intellectual work of philosophy might be devoted to arguing for, analysing, defending or attacking these premises, but the process is still deductive. As a scientist, my training is to use empirical logic: to observe what occurs and seek rules or explanations that fit a range of observations. This approach can be applied to ethics by asking how normal people consider the ethics of an issue. I believe that it is crucially important to address the ethics of animal experimentation in this way as well. It may not help us find any ruling moral principles, but it will help us understand the normal, everyday ethics of animal experimentation.

Summarising the arguments

Earlier in this chapter, when addressing the question of whether we have a right to experiment on animals, I attempted to define some of the qualities of a 'right'. I noted that to deny someone a right was to deny him or her something that is intrinsic or important to his or her nature or existence. On that quality alone one might argue that animals have rights, since there are clearly things that are intrinsic to their existence. However, there are other equally important aspects of rights. I also mentioned that rights are generally regarded as having concomitant responsibilities. This would rule out the idea of animals having rights as they cannot recognise or exercise responsibilities or duties. If, for the sake of argument, humans extended rights to animals, animals would not and could not extend rights to humans. This makes the concept of animal rights seem irrational.

There are obviously limitations to this argument. Human society extends essentially the same rights to rational, healthy adults, to newborn babies and to patients in a coma, despite the fact that the latter two groups are clearly unable to exercise responsibilities. However, the inclusion of such groups is based on the expectation that, in the case of babies, they will become able to exercise responsibilities and, in the case of coma patients, they previously were able and may regain that ability to exercise responsibilities. There are cases where humans cannot ever realistically be likely to exercise responsibilities – e.g. anencephalic babies or coma patients in a persistent vegetative state. If we automatically extend the same rights to such humans as we do to all others, which is an issue worthy of debate in itself, we might be guilty of doing so for sentimental rather than logical reasons. However, such a very limited exception from the rule does not undermine an argument based on the normal case.

Another way of considering this question is to ask whether animals would have rights if human beings ceased to exist. In this 'back in the jungle' argument, it is clear that the notion of animal rights is meaningless. Without humans, rights would have no effect whatsoever on animals. In this sense, rights are merely a human invention.

Regan (1983) argues that animals have inherent value since they are 'the experiencing subject of a life'. He argues that all living animals have equal value and thus equal rights. However, even if we accept the first part of this argument, the second – that animals have equal value and thus rights – gives rise to far too many absurd conclusions to be accepted. Do parasitic nematodes in our gut have the same rights as us? If so, since there are so many of them, should their collective rights overwhelm ours?

Singer's utilitarian arguments against using animals rest on the premise that the ability to experience suffering is the defining quality for including something in the utilitarian calculus. He adheres to an approach that does not differentiate between humans and non-human animals at all. Strict utilitarianism leads to conclusions that the vast majority would find unacceptable if not reprehensible, even without considering the involvement of animals. For example, utilitarianism would regard it as acceptable to kill a severely disabled baby to allow a healthy baby to survive. If several lives can be saved by using different organs from a single person for transplantation, utilitarianism would regard the killing of the donor as morally right.

Singer, like Regan, regards non-human animals as morally equivalent to humans and his arguments have the same problems in this regard. The normal world is replete with examples of unavoidable conflicts between the interests of humans and the interests of non-human animals. Who should we evict from the tenements, the humans or the rats? Almost everyone would regard it as wrong to evict the humans, so we clearly do not consider there to be any equality of rights between humans and other animals.

If we reject Singer's and Regan's arguments for the complete abolition of animal experimentation, what can we put in their place? Instead of arguing from basic principles (animal rights or utilitarianism), we can turn the analysis around and ask: what is normally done in this area of human activity, what ethical judgements are made and what are the underlying moral principles involved? For the purposes of this argument, I use the term 'normal person' to describe the position taken on these issues by the majority of people in Western, developed countries, using the UK as the prototype (Davies, 2000; Coghlan *et al.*, 1999).

Leaving aside those who take an animal rights or antivivisection view of this issue, the ethical position on animal experimentation taken by most people is to accept that it should be done for important medical research, but to want the use of animals and any suffering involved to be kept to a minimum. Clearly, this view places human interests above those of the animals, which is consistent with the ethical position that the majority of people take on other uses of animals. Most people in Western countries consider it acceptable to eat meat, i.e. to use animals as a source of human food. Many of these people will be aware that eating meat is not necessary – since people can live on a vegetarian diet – and so they should accept that they are using animals for pleasure and convenience, rather than for any greater need.

Does this mean that the majority of people place no value upon the lives of animals? Almost certainly not. If a normal person could decide whether an animal should be painlessly killed or allowed to live, with no other consequences, they would normally let the animal live. Our empathic response to death is that it is a bad thing. This view is supported by the fact that, when it comes to animal experiments, the normal person wants to see the minimum number of animals used (and killed) apparently as a separate consideration from reducing any suffering to a minimum. From this we can conclude that people do regard animal lives as having a value, but this value is much less than that of human lives.

How, then, does the normal person regard animal suffering? Their demand that any suffering involved in animal experiments be kept to a minimum acknowledges that animals do have interests (i.e. the avoidance of suffering) that should be protected. Indeed, the requirement that animals are only used (and thus exposed to the risk of suffering) for important purposes indicates that, if anything, people seem to be more concerned about animals suffering than about animals dying.

The balancing of human interests against animal interests is essentially a utilitarian process, seeking the greatest good or pleasure. However, it measures good or pleasure on different scales for humans and animals. There may well be a range of scales that the normal person operates. Does the life and well-being of a slug have the same importance or value as that of a chimpanzee? Most people would say not. They seem to apply an importance to the interests of an animal that is based either on its sentience or on how close it is to humans.

Since human interests can so easily override animal interests, the normal person clearly does not believe that animals have rights. However, most people would accept that we humans have some rights. This gives us a picture of an ethical system in which animals have no rights but have clear interests which should be protected. However, those interests are weighed against human and other interests in a utilitarian manner.

In practical terms, the protection of the interests of animals used in experiments is based on the principles of the three Rs – reduce, replace, refine – defined by Russell and Burch. They argued that all animal experimentation should seek to reduce the number of animals used in any experiment to the minimum necessary for meaningful results, replace animal experiments with alternative, *in vitro* systems whenever possible and refine the way animal experiments are conducted to minimise any pain, suffering or distress caused (Russell and Burch, 1959). The three Rs are now widely accepted as the basic ethical principles of laboratory animal welfare.

Questions raised and useful concepts

The debate about the ethics of using animals in medical research raises several important questions. I have tried to answer those questions, but I readily acknowledge that others will find different answers to them. Thus, the more important part of this essay may not be the answers I have offered, but the questions that have been defined.

The concept of animal rights looms large in this debate and so the question of the nature of rights is central to the debate. The nature of rights will strongly influence whether animals are seen as having rights. If they can have rights, do they have them in the same way that humans have rights? Or, as I have tried to suggest, is the concept of rights an inappropriate tool for considering these issues?

I have used the concept of interests to consider the moral standing of animals and have dealt with those interests in a broadly utilitarian manner. However, there are some subtle issues with regard to the way that interests should be weighed, for example when different species are being compared. How do we know when one interest outweighs another? A strict utilitarian approach would ask which produces the greater good or pleasure. This raises the question of how we weigh human pleasure against animal pleasure, how we weigh our pleasure against animal pain and how we compare something that is 'good' for humans with something that is 'merely' pleasurable.

The concept of the three Rs (reduce, replace and refine) as the practical ethical principles of laboratory animal welfare is well known to those who use animals in research and testing. They are used as the basic principles of most systems of regulating animal experimentation around the world. In this sense, they fit well with the moral position taken by the broad majority of people on this issue, and I have attempted to analyse the nature of this moral position.

In this analysis I have offered for consideration what might be called 'everyday ethics': an attempt to analyse how normal, reasonably well-informed people in the Western world think ethically about this issue. The result is a mixture of rights-based thinking (for some human issues) set in a broad background of practical utilitarianism. In this setting animals are not seen as having rights, but they have important interests that should be protected, sometimes at the cost of human pleasure. However, it is clear that human interests are always regarded as more important than animal interests.

References

Anon. (1863) *The Lancet* ii, pp. 252–3.

Bliss, M. (1983) *The Discovery of Insulin* (Edinburgh, Paul Harris).

Coghlan, A., Copley, J. and Aldhous, P. (1999) Let the people speak, *New Scientist*, 22 May.

Davies, B. (2000) In-depth survey of public attitudes shows surprising degree of acceptance. *RDS News*, April, 8–11.

Florey, H. (1953) *Conquest* 41, pp. 4–22.

French, R.D. (1975) *Antivivisection and Medical Science in Victorian Society* (Princetown, USA, Princetown University Press).

Gay, W.I. (1987) *Health Benefits of Animal Research* (Washington, DC, Foundation for Biomedical Research).

Maehle, A-H. and Trohler, U. (1987) Animal experimentation from antiquity to the end of the eighteenth century: attitudes and arguments, in Rupke, N.A. (Ed.) *Vivisection in Historical Perspective* (Kent, UK, Croom-Helm).

Manuel, D. (1987) Marshall Hall (1790–1857): Vivisection and the development of experimental physiology, in Rupke, N.A. (Ed.) *Vivisection in Historical Perspective* (Kent, UK, Croom-Helm).

Regan, T. (1983) *The Case for Animal Rights* (Berkeley, University of California Press).

Research Defence Society (RDS) (undated) Anaesthetics at http://www.rds-online. org.uk/milestones/anaes.html#inhale

Rhodes, P. (1985) *An Outline of the History of Medicine* (London, Butterworths).

Russell, W. and Burch, R. (1959) *The Principles of Humane Experimental Technique* (London, Methuen).

Sharpe, R. (1988) *The Cruel Deception* (Northamptonshire, Thorsons).

Singer, P. (1976) *Animal Liberation* (London, Jonathan Cape).

Further information sources

The Research Defence Society (RDS) website (www.rds-online.org.uk) contains detailed information about the use of animals in medical research.

Sir Willam Paton's 1993 book *Man and Mouse* (Oxford University Press) remains the best general discussion of why animals are used in medical research and testing.

A thorough and considered appraisal of the debate about animal experimentation can be found in Professor Andrew Rowan's 1995 book *The Animal Research Contro-versy* (Centre for Animals and Public Policy, Tufts University School of Veterinary Medicine).

Biography

Mark Matfield trained and worked as a medical research scientist in the UK and USA. Since 1988 he has been Executive Director of the Research Defence Society, the main organisation in the UK representing the scientific community in the public and political debate about the use of animals in medical research and testing. He has written and lectured widely on the public understanding of, and public attitudes to, animal experimentation.

17 The case against the use of animals in medical experiments

Gill Langley

Animal experimentation as a scientific method began to gain currency in Britain in the nineteenth century, with the spread of the new disciplines of experimental physiology and medicine. There was adverse public reaction to the suffering endured by animals, as well as to the conditions in which they were kept. Anaesthetics were discovered in the late 1840s, but for many years they were not always used even for prolonged and invasive surgery. The indifference of some scientists to animal suffering led, in 1876, to a law being passed in Britain which controlled the more severe excesses.

For a century and a half animal experimentation became a dominant methodology in medical research. It's easy to see why. Scientists wanted to know more about the living body, but ethically they could not conduct their experiments on people. Other animals were considered the next best thing: living surrogates or 'models' – albeit imperfect – of human beings, with few ethical constraints on their exploitation. By the mid-1970s the number of experiments conducted each year in Britain rose to a peak of 5.6 million.

Because animal research has been a major strand of scientific endeavour for so long, many medical advances have involved experiments on animals. However, simply because animal experiments have figured in many medical developments does not necessarily mean that every advance has benefited from animal experiments or crucially depended on them. It would also be incorrect simply to assume that, because animal experiments were so widely used in the last two centuries, they must remain a dominant methodology in the twenty-first century.

Do we have the right to use animals in medical research?

The moral status of animals is at the centre of ethical debate about whether we have the right to use them in research and testing. Few people disagree that animals count in our moral framework. The more difficult question, especially in the case of animal research, is how much do they count? Should the needs and interests of other animals weigh as heavily in the balance as those of humans?

The key issue here is the capacity to suffer. Some organisms' reactions are solely reflexive and without subjective experience. This is the case, for example, with bacteria, which have simple reflexes which cause them to swim towards favourable stimuli and away from toxic ones. If an organism does not consciously experience pain because it lacks the higher faculties needed to generate feelings of suffering and distress (i.e. it is not sentient), then we need not be concerned about causing it individual harm.

However, the animals used in medical research – such as mice, rats, guinea pigs, rabbits, dogs, cats and monkeys – *are* sentient. It is accepted that they have the capacity to experience 'pain, distress, suffering or lasting harm', to use the precise wording of the current British law on animal experiments. Like us, they have pain receptors, nerves which conduct pain signals to the brain and regions of the brain which elaborate on these signals and generate unpleasant experiences. If scientists believed that animals do not feel pain, they would not use them in pain research or in the development of pain-relieving drugs intended for human use. But they do.

The capacity of animals to experience pain is sufficient reason, in the eyes of many, to refrain on moral grounds from harming them, even in the name of medical progress. After all, this is precisely the principle which constrains people from condoning painful experiments on non-consenting humans. It is unethical to do so because we know that other people, like us, feel pain and distress. Exactly the same argument should logically apply to other animals.

Beyond pain sensation, though, lie questions of mental complexity which also impact on the moral status of animals. There is persuasive evidence that some animals – mammals and probably birds – have thoughts, feelings, memories and intentions. These attributes are morally significant because it means that other animals can, like us, be harmed not just by pain but also by confinement, frustration, maternal deprivation, fear, isolation and, of course, loss of life. These kinds of experiences are unavoidable for animals confined in laboratories and used in experiments.

The measurement of stress hormones in animals, and studies of the adverse consequences of pain and stress in laboratory animals – such as psychological and behavioural abnormalities, ulcers, brain dysfunction, immune suppression and heart damage – provide further evidence that the animals commonly used in laboratories do suffer pain and distress (Manser, 1992). Laws and regulations controlling animal experiments around the world are based on this understanding.

Disciplines such as animal ethology, cognitive psychology and evolutionary biology combine to show that there is an evolutionary continuum of mental and emotional functions throughout the animal kingdom, rather than a major discontinuity between humans and all other species (Rodd, 1990). Ethologists have painstakingly observed and recorded the behaviour of animals in their natural habitats. Their work has helped to fuel a revolution in our understanding of the mental (as well as social and cultural) complexities of animals.

The two key philosophical challenges to the status quo have their roots in utilitarianism and animal rights. The philosopher Peter Singer takes a utilitarian approach, applying a cost/benefit analysis to animal research but on the basis that, in the case of sentient animals, there must be genuine equality of consideration across the species (Singer, 1975). Singer has argued that occasionally it may be ethically more acceptable to experiment on a severely brain-damaged human infant with no subjective awareness than on a healthy chimpanzee. A comparison of this kind does force us to think deeply about whether animals are treated justly and whether the information which might be obtained from an experiment is worth acquiring at the cost in suffering.

Interestingly, in the last few years Britain and New Zealand have implemented *de facto* bans on experiments on chimpanzees (and the other great apes), and the Dutch government has announced its intention to do so. The Dutch announcement brings to an end chimpanzee research which had been underway for many years. These decisions were based primarily on an acceptance of the moral status of the great apes, and represent a changing moral climate.

The second philosophical challenge comes from Tom Regan, who has developed an animal rights philosophy based on the principle that some animals other than humans not only feel pain but also have awareness, thoughts, memories, intentions and anticipations (Regan, 1983). He calls them 'subjects of a life, with a biography as well as a biology', and argues that these animals have inherent moral value independent of their usefulness to us. Some people counter that only individuals who have duties can have rights; but human individuals who have no duties – whether because of age (babies or the very elderly) or infirmity (such as mental disorders) – are not stripped of their rights. Tom Regan's position is that animal (and human) experimentation is wrong in principle and should not be permitted, regardless of any benefits which it may bring.

Knowing what we know about other animals, what are the rational arguments for granting *all* humans a higher moral status than *all* other animals? If we are against painful experiments on non-consenting humans because of the suffering which would be caused, we should oppose experiments on other sentient animals too.

Those who argue that benefits to society justify experiments on animals must consider that the results of similar experiments on people would be much more relevant and reliable and therefore more likely to be genuinely beneficial. Does that justify painful experiments on humans? Apparently not, but why not? Is it because in this case utilitarianism is easy to apply to animals but not so acceptable in the human situation? These lines of thought tend to give weight to the human/animal rights approach, that is, that certain things are wrong in principle, regardless of potentially beneficial outcomes.

This is not, of course, the prevailing attitude to the use of animals in medical research and testing. Although public opinion polls increasingly suggest that most ordinary people are opposed, in principle, to animal experimentation, the scientific and political view is that animals' pain and distress do count, but not as heavily as human interests. Thus, animals should not be made to suffer in laboratories for frivolous reasons, they should not be used in excessive numbers or subjected to 'unnecessary' pain, and non-animal alternative methods should be employed where possible. This orthodox view results in an estimated 100 million sentient animals being used in scientific procedures worldwide every year.

Genetic modification and xenotransplantation

Although still high, the number of experiments on animals has been falling since the 1970s and 1980s. Annual figures in most countries are now some 30–50 per cent lower than at their peak.

This has come about through changing attitudes, leading to stricter regulation, and through the development of techniques which replace animal use. However, unless difficult decisions are made in the near future, there is a risk that these trends will start to reverse. The genetic modification of animals is a growth area and has increased enormously: in Britain by 1,200 per cent between 1990 and 2000. This increase is starting to reverse the overall decline in animal use. But there is more at stake than a justifiable concern about numbers of animals: the genetic modification of animals raises serious ethical and practical issues.

Firstly, there is the argument that deliberately altering the 'blueprint' of animals' lives – their DNA – may be wrong in itself, regardless of the consequences. But the key issue is the effect on the animals themselves. Genetic modification can cause sudden, traumatic and unpredictable changes in animals which can cause pain, suffering and death (Wheale and McNally, 1995). The genes used may have been artificially modified or have derived from a completely different species (including bacteria, viruses and plants). Unexpected effects occur because certain aspects of genetic modification cannot be precisely controlled and because of a lack of understanding of how genes interact (with each other and with environmental factors) to influence the development of an animal. The process by which genetically modified animals are produced is also inherently wasteful: it requires the use of tens or hundreds of animals in order to achieve a desired transgenic strain.

Increasingly, science is being driven by commercial enterprises, whose powerful economic interests sometimes conflict with public opinion and policy. Two commercial exploitations of genetic engineering – the development of animals as 'bioreactors' for the production of therapeutic proteins and as sources of organs for transplantation – seem particularly likely to escalate animal use.

When genetic modification became a practical proposition, it became possible to modify plants, cell cultures or animals so that they would manufacture medically important proteins. These proteins may be antibodies, vaccines or human proteins which can alleviate certain medical conditions (such as blood clotting factors in haemophilia). Despite laws meant to provide some protection of animals' interests and requiring non-animal methods to be used when available, most commercial companies aggressively pursued the animal option, perceiving it as the most profitable.

In particular, animals such as rabbits, sheep, goats and cattle have been genetically modified to produce human proteins in their milk. Again, because genetic modification is an inefficient technology, many animals' lives have been wasted in efforts to produce the desired transgenic strains. In several instances considerable suffering occurred when the protein of interest (e.g. human growth hormone) was also produced in tissues other than the mammary glands or leaked into the bloodstream, with toxic effects on the animals. Yet it is also very practical and economic to genetically modify plants for these purposes, and there are signs that some companies now realise this and may change their production systems from animals to plants. On ethical and legislative grounds, this should have been their first choice.

The genetic modification of animals to provide compatible organs for transplantation into humans (xenotransplantation) is another contentious area of medical research. Like the protein production example, xenotransplantation research is based on a view of animals as production systems rather than as sentient beings. And again, commercial companies are driving forward a new field of research, with inadequate reflection on ethical aspects or alternative strategies.

Thousands of animals have already been used in xenotransplantation research without it even being known whether an animal organ can function in the human body and sustain human life in the long term (Langley and D'Silva, 1998). Other approaches to bridging the organ gap, such as modifying the (human) organ donation system and boosting the resources available to transplant co-ordinators and intensive care teams, have been ignored in many countries in favour of invasive, high-tech research on animals. The experiments have involved genetic modification of pigs, major surgery in primates (and other animals), treatment with toxic drugs, organ rejection and death. The idea is that the pigs can be altered so that their organs, otherwise perceived by the human body as foreign, will not be so easily rejected. So far the research, which was trumpeted as the solution to organ shortages, has failed to deliver the expected benefits.

Contributions – setting the terms of the debate

Within the context of the current system of regulation of animal experiments, there are several key issues which underpin the debate.

The effectiveness of animal research

Many people argue in favour of animal experimentation on the general assumption that it is a valid approach to solving human medical problems. However, in certain fields it is clear that problems with the reliability and relevance of animal experiments exist but have not been addressed.

A case in point is the testing of chemicals and medicines on animals in an effort to ensure that they will be safe for human use. Animal tests are conducted to check for adverse effects such as eye irritancy, skin allergy, acute poisoning, cancer risk (carcinogenicity) or genetic damage. Some of the test methods are more than fifty years old, and are based on outdated science, for example using subjectively measured endpoints which make it difficult to obtain consistent results.

When the animal methods were developed, it was assumed that the results of tests on guinea pigs, mice, rats and dogs would be applicable to humans, but experience has shown that this is not always the case. The extrapolation is technically difficult, partly because of the need to factor in differences in body weight, volume and life span between animals and humans, but also because the way test animals and humans are exposed to substances varies (e.g. in magnitude and frequency of dosing). Additionally, there can be significant variation in results depending on the species chosen for the test, and even among different strains of the same species. To illustrate, a recent international collaborative study found that where the same chemicals had been tested twice in rodent cancer-risk tests, the results were the same only in 57 per cent of cases.

Problems with animal experiments are also apparent in a number of fields of medical research, especially in the use of animal 'models' of human conditions, which range from multiple sclerosis and kidney failure to stroke and septic shock. Most human illnesses do not occur naturally in laboratory animals, so they are often created artificially by chemical, genetic or surgical means. Because of this, their similarities to the human illness can be very limited. Additionally, animals used as surrogates for humans may not have the same metabolism, biochemistry, physiology or even anatomy, so that results are difficult to interpret. For example, there has been a long and intense research effort to develop new therapies to treat the effects of stroke. More than 25 new drugs have proved successful in animal models of stroke but none were safe and effective in human patients.

By any ethical standards, whether animal rights-based or utilitarian, experiments on animals should not be permitted when there is evidence that they are faulty in design or misleading in outcome. An alternative approach is to seek methods which do not involve animal experiments: such techniques can be supported by all sides of the vivisection debate.

The necessity of animal research

The concept of non-animal methods was taken forward in practical terms by anti-vivisection organisations, which established humane research charities in the 1960s and 1970s. These charities have funded the development and application of techniques such as cell culture, computer modelling, molecular studies and volunteer research specifically to replace animal experiments, at a time when governments, scientists and mainstream funding bodies were dismissive even of the possibility.

Since then non-animal research methods have gained credibility and expert support. Some countries have national centres for this kind of work and many governments provide budgets earmarked for replacing animal experiments. A number of test tube-based tests have been officially accepted as valid in recent years (such as a cellular assay for detecting light-induced skin irritation, and the human skin model for skin corrosion which replaces the use of rabbits in painful tests). A growing number of scientists believe that, by implementing modern techniques into non-animal methodologies, better science could be done than with laboratory animals.

Despite an ethical imperative to spare animals from laboratory suffering, the major funding bodies and professional scientific societies have not enthusiastically embraced the non-animal research approach. Perhaps there is a remnant here of the old-fashioned scientific arrogance which held that science is ethically neutral, and that scientists should be free from interference to follow their chosen directions.

The regulation of animal research

A crucial aspect of the Animals (Scientific Procedures) Act, which controls animal experiments in Britain, is the requirement to conduct a cost/benefit assessment. This is a utilitarian approach which attempts to perform a balancing act between the potential 'costs' to animals (in terms of pain and suffering) and the potential benefits to humans. Only if the sum of human benefits is likely to outweigh the costs to animals should a research project using animals be given a licence by the Secretary of State.

However, the parameters of the assessment are set so as to favour humans. The purposes for which animals are permitted to be experimented on include not only medical progress, but also a simple increase in biological knowledge which may have no immediate practical use at all. In this kind of basic or fundamental research, with only tentative future benefits or perhaps none at all, it is difficult to see how the cost/benefit assessment can lead to approval of experiments which cause suffering to animals. Worryingly, government statistics show that, contrary to the overall trend of decreasing numbers, the use of animals in fundamental research has not fallen since the Animals (Scientific Procedures) Act was passed in 1986.

Certain kinds of licence are issued to cover very large programmes of animal testing, involving hundreds of animals in toxicity tests of a wide range of products. Commercial testing laboratories bid for contracts to test products which range from new drugs to low-calorie sweeteners or household chemicals. How does the Secretary of State judge the benefits of such testing programmes when he has no idea which particular products a contract laboratory may test over the coming years?

Commercial gain should not be a justification for using animals in experiments. Yet few countries have a system to prevent two rival companies independently testing a new chemical or drug on hundreds of animals. Neither do regulations require a company to share its data with another, even on payment of a fee, in order to prevent duplicate testing. Two pharmaceutical companies may quite separately be working on very similar lines to develop a new animal 'model' of a human disease. The Home Office, which regulates animal experiments in Britain, could be aware of such duplication but would not inform the companies or propose that the companies work together on certain aspects of the research to minimise animal suffering.

International considerations

We live in a global society, and the international nature and regulation of many human activities has a bearing on the use of animals in medical research.

In Europe animal experiments are regulated not only by national legislation but also by European laws. European Directive 86/609/EEC requires all member states to ensure that animals' pain and distress is minimised, and that animals are not used where satisfactory non-animal methods are available. In fact it goes further and requires that member states should encourage research into the development of non-animal methods and procedures which minimise harm to animals – although European countries differ in the zeal with which they implement these legislative requirements.

Despite this European Directive, in some quarters it has been suggested that a single country should not 'unilaterally' prohibit an animal test for which a valid non-animal alternative exists, because of the 'harmonised market'. This would result in animals being used unnecessarily in tests throughout Europe until the slowest member state implemented the alternative method. A more ethical approach would be for member states who are ahead of others in these respects to pro-actively persuade their European partners to follow suit.

World Trade Organisation (WTO) and related trade agreements may increasingly have an impact on animal experiment issues. The WTO strictly limits the extent to which nations can restrict trade on the basis of ethical concerns, such as the protection of people, animals or the environment. For example, a WTO member probably could not ban the import of goods produced or tested by methods contrary to its own laws. The problem has already arisen in the European Union in respect of cosmetics: despite the wishes of the Parliament to ban the import of cosmetics tested on animals, the Commission is taking the view that this cannot be done for fear of a challenge under WTO rules.

Another ongoing example involves the production of special antibodies used widely in medical research and diagnosis. These monoclonal antibodies have traditionally been produced in living animals by a procedure (the ascites method) which can be painful and distressing. Several countries have now accepted test-tube production methods as a humane alternative, and have banned or severely restricted the use of animals on their own territory.

However, a loophole exists: scientists can still buy commercial, animal-produced antibodies from overseas suppliers. It is unlikely that an attempt to ban the import of inhumanely produced antibodies, or even to require them to be labelled as 'animal-produced', would be permitted under the WTO rules. A concerted effort needs to be made to ensure that trade agreements do permit restrictions on ethical grounds, whether to benefit animals, people or the environment.

Summarising the arguments and useful concepts

The reason people object to the use of humans in forcible experiments is that we wish to refrain from causing them unjust suffering, even if society as a whole might benefit. Human individuals have inherent moral value and consequently a right not to be used in an instrumental manner. Since the available evidence indicates that other animals also experience pain and distress, why do not the same principles apply to them? Belonging to a particular species does not automatically confer moral superiority; anthropocentric views are as irrational and immoral as racist or sexist stances.

The moral climate regarding experiments on animals has changed radically in the last twenty years, and will continue to evolve as we learn more about their sentiency and mental capacities. Growing public awareness and concern has led to stricter control of animal experimentation, a steady reduction in animal use, and investment in the development of techniques to replace animal use. There are areas of research where non-animal methods could be developed, and other areas where animal use is notably unreliable or non-predictive. In these cases there is an ethical imperative, as well as a legislative impetus, to follow the alternative approaches and not to conduct the experiments on animals.

There is a risk that humane advances made in recent years may be slowed, both by the explosive growth of animal genetic modification and by multinational corporations driving scientific research in profitable directions without adequate public debate. Commercial and world trade pressures should not be permitted to override fundamental ethical principles.

It is important to realise that moral standards are not merely the preserve of philosophers or governments, and neither are they set in stone. Everyone has a part to play in thinking about and commenting on the issues. Although it's difficult for an individual to influence national or world affairs, we can make a difference in our own lives and influence friends and colleagues.

References

Langley, G. and D'Silva, J. (1998) *Animal Organs in Humans: Uncalculated Risks and Unanswered Questions* (London and Petersfield, British Union for the Abolition of Vivisection and Compassion in World Farming).
Manser, C. E. (1992) *The Assessment of Stress in Laboratory Animals* (Horsham, RSPCA).

Regan, T. (1983) *The Case for Animal Rights* (California, University of California Press).
Rodd, R. (1990) *Biology, Ethics and Animals* (Oxford, Oxford University Press).
Singer, P. (1975) *Animal Liberation* (New York, Avon).
Wheale, P. and McNally, R. (1995) *Animal Genetic Engineering: Of Pigs, Oncomice and Men* (London, Pluto Press).

Further reading

Bekoff, M. (Ed.) (1998) *Encyclopedia of Animal Rights and Animal Welfare* (Connecticut, Greenwood Press).
Hundreds of entries by different contributors, alphabetically arranged by subject and including animal cognition, alternatives to animal experiments, pain, religion and animals, and other animal issues.

Garner, R. (1993) *Animals, Politics and Morality* (Manchester and New York, Manchester University Press).
A detailed overview of the moral issues and political debate on animal rights, with emphasis on medical research, agriculture and conservation.

Grayson, L. (2000) *Animals in Research: For and Against* (London, The British Library). This is an independent review of the subject and also a resource book containing hundreds of references to literature on the topic.

The Dr Hadwen Trust website (www.drhadwentrust.org.uk) provides information about non-animal alternatives to animal experiments.
The British Union for the Abolition of Vivisection website (www.buav.org) includes a range of animal experimentation factsheets, covering issues such as drug testing, genetic modification and patenting.

Biography

Gill Langley gained her PhD in natural sciences at Cambridge University and is a long-standing animal rights advocate. She works as scientific adviser to the Dr Hadwen Trust for Humane Research, a charity which funds non-animal medical research, and has lectured and published widely. She is also a freelance consultant for anti-vivisection and animal protection organisations in Europe and the USA.

Index